PICTURING GOD

Norman Pittenger

PICTURING
GOD

SCM PRESS LTD

334 01260 0

First published 1982
by SCM Press Ltd
58 Bloomsbury Street London WC1

Phototypeset by Input Typesetting Ltd
Printed and bound in Great Britain at
The Camelot Press Ltd, Southampton

This book is dedicated to three friends,
all devout priests in the Roman Catholic Church,
learned scholars and exemplars of true *amicitia*:
JOSEPH WILLIAM GOETZ
DONALD GOERGEN, OP
BERNARD LEE, SM

Contents

Preface

The chapters of this book were originally delivered as part of a series of lectures at the 1980 summer school of the Benedictine-sponsored St John's University in Collegeville, Minnesota, in the United States. The material was repeated in 1981 at Christian Theological Seminary in Indiana. I have retained the style appropriate to lectures, rather than re-write the material in a more formal and academic style, in the hope that what is here presented in this fashion may be more 'available' to ordinary educated women and men.

As I urge in the first chapter, there can be no doubt that today, even more than when Whitehead said it, the big question in religious (and often also in secular) discussion is 'What do we mean by "God"?' Those who affirm God and those who deny him must always ask exactly how they are 'modelling' God. Certainly much is said or implied that makes the word 'God' entirely unacceptable; in this book I explore some of the reasons for this unacceptability. But if we cannot 'do' with much that is found in the hitherto common portrayal of God, neither can we 'do' without that which, or him who, is supremely worshipful, utterly dependable, and unsurpassable by anything not himself or itself. We cannot 'do' without the one who 'will not let us go', however much we may seek to escape from that divine reality, the one who alone can provide human life with final significance and abiding value amid 'the changes and chances' that mark our existence as men and women in this finite world.

Fortunately the possibility of a more satisfactory model for God is offered to us today, thanks to the influence of the conceptuality enunciated by Alfred North Whitehead and others during the past half-century or so. Increasingly this approach is being adopted by many theologians in the Christian world, not least in the Roman Catholic church (of which St John's University is a distinguished institution), but also in the Reformed denominations. I have sought to present here, in as direct and simple a fashion as I can manage, what the concept, which I have called the new model, affirms. Yet I am convinced that this way of seeing God is also in *one* sense the *point* of the old model, since its basic affirmation is grounded in the witness to God in Christ about which the New Testament tells us.

I express my gratitude especially for the attention and interest which was shown by the priests, seminarians, and religious who heard the lectures at St John's University. My weeks at that university were happy and refreshing. I also thank faculty and students at Christian Theological Seminary in Indianapolis for their hospitality and friendship.

1

Introduction: Models and their Function. The Grounds for Faith

In a book published more than fifty years ago, the Anglo-American philosopher Alfred North Whitehead (see note on Whitehead on page xx) wrote these words: 'Today there is but one religious dogma in debate: What do you mean by "God"? And in this respect, today is like all its yesterdays. This is the fundamental religious dogma, and all other dogmas are subsidiary to it.' (*Religion in the Making*, New American Library 1926, p. 66). The 'today' to which Whitehead referred was in 1926, but it could just as well be in this present year. There is indeed but one issue – he called it 'dogma' – which matters above all others in the religious dimension: when we use the ancient and hallowed word 'God', what are we pointing to, what are we getting at, what are we talking about?

A few pages later in the same book Whitehead made this striking comment, also entirely appropriate for our day: 'The modern world has lost God and is seeking him.' If that was true in 1926, it is even more true today. The 'loss of God' is obvious to us all; and the search for him, while it may not be quite so obvious, is going on wherever human beings are deeply concerned with the meaning or significance of their existence and are trying, sometimes with a desperate yearning, to find a basis or ground for their confidence in living in the face of all that threatens them and that could destroy them and their achievements.

Whitehead's two observations belong together. For I am sure that the chief reason for the 'loss of God' is to be found in the absence of a conception of God which makes sense to men and women and which does not offend their highest sensibility nor deny the knowledge they possess. If the word 'God' denotes for them that which does thus offend and deny, they can do nothing other than reject it. On the other hand, if there is a conception of God which does neither of these, but which expresses that sensibility and is in accordance with that knowledge, they may well be able to accept it joyfully.

It is my own conviction that just such a conception is today available, possessing sufficient continuity with former views to make the use of the vocable 'God' permissible, but yet sufficiently different from much that has been said in the past to make it genuinely meaningful in our own time. This book will seek to present such a conception; and in presenting it, will sum up a good deal of what has been going on in the world of religious experience and thought during the past half-century or so.

The term 'conception' has been used several times in the last few paragraphs. But I prefer to use another word: model. When we use the word 'God', what model – that is, what symbol or picture – do we have in mind? Model is a helpful term that is increasingly used in many theoretical discussions, in science above all, to provide a focal centre for thinking and, in consequence, a guide to action. Without some such focus for thought and guide to action, we humans seem unable to proceed about our business. What is more, the model which we adopt determines to a considerable degree the possibility for a particular type of experience. Some models can inhibit us, more especially if they make nonsense of what we know and understand more generally; others can open up for us a new possibility for living and acting.

In our next two chapters we shall look at what has become in Western thought the dominant model that is in mind when the word 'God' is employed. We shall also see how that model has failed us, for reasons that will be adduced. In consequence, the continued insistence on maintaining that model has made any significant religious orientation well-nigh impossible for many people today, at least in a conscious manner. So we have heard that 'God is dead'; and as one of the advocates of that position once put it, this has meant not that many have a feeling of the 'absence' of God, but that they have no notion of *God as being absent*. There is for them no opportunity to know the sort of experience which would give meaning to the word God; on the contrary, there is simple negation. The old model has died on them and they have known no other which could be put in its place and thus provide something positive to which they could react.

If a religious model is no longer available to them many will look for and find something else that can serve much the same purpose.

This is the truth in Luther's well-known contention that a man's god is 'what he worships' or serves. And such a god need not be anything which commonly we should think of calling 'divine'.

This was brought home to me very vividly a number of years ago during a long discussion with a friend who was a convinced communist. He accepted, with what could be styled almost a religious fervour, the dialectical materialism developed out of Marx by Lenin and other communist theorists. This pattern, in which humanity through the class struggle is moving towards realization of a classless society, with its wider implications of a world-process which is similarly an ongoing evolution of matter but yet is not old-fashioned nineteenth century 'materialism', provided for him the 'master-light of all his seeing'. What is more, it gave him a basis for action as a devoted and busy member of the 'party'. In other words, it was the model in terms of which he saw everything and did everything.

We talked about a number of questions which to me seemed of great importance, such as death and its significance, deep human relationships like friendship, love, marriage, and other matters. It was interesting to see how he looked at and understood each of these through his accepted model. Some issues were simply dismissed because they did not fit into the organizing scheme. For example, his attitude towards death was a refusal to see its utter seriousness as a matter of existential awareness; for him death was simply a plain fact which, once the classless society had come about, would no longer be of much concern to anyone. So also with the experience of love and human relationships of all sorts. What was for him the significant point was always whether or not this or that sort of contact contributed towards the realization of the Marxist goal. He simply could not see, hence he could not know in his own experience, what the human race generally has both seen and known, and what the great literature of the world has related in novel and poem and play, about the quality of depth in such relationships; or about death as not only the end of human life but as an indication of life's 'finality' (to use Heidegger's idiom); and above all about the possibility of a cosmic anchorage for the human sense of meaning or value in experience. If ever he were to grasp any of this, I concluded, he would need a change of model or, at the very least, such a modification of the one he accepted that room might be found for these aspects or areas of life.

My friend's attitude here was not simply intellectual. It included his emotional life with its feeling-tones and it was accepted with some sort of imaginative grasp that went beyond mere rational assent. It is for this reason that I prefer to speak in this book of model rather than of conception. The latter is far and away too intellectual, too rational, too much a matter of theory or speculation. However useful that may be, we surely see that in any area of human experience, once we have got beyond the strictly scientific (and even there, if some recent authorities are to be believed, more than intellectual agreement is required when some master-idea is taken as vital in one's experimental or observational work), we are in the realm of imagination. Coleridge made this point years ago. And John Keats' well-known adage. 'we think on our pulses', is highly relevant.

A model, then, has an intellectual component but it is much more profoundly a matter of deeply-felt acceptance. Above all this is the case when we consider the abiding sense of meaning, worth, significance, or value, felt in human experience. To put it simply, we usually assume that 'life is worth living'; the prejudice against easy suicide is a sign of this assumption. Of course such a profound feeling need not always be entertained in a vivid and highly conscious fashion; it may persist deep down in our lives but in a vague manner, only very occasionally coming to the surface and requiring some sort of expression in a moment of great elation or great depression. But none the less, it is there; and it is there all the time. But what grounds that sense of worth? Just here we need a model.

It was to emphasize this imaginative and emotional side of our experience that I used other words such as 'picture' and 'symbol' with the term 'model'. For these bring out the supra-intellectual in such dominating conceptions as I intend here to indicate. A picture appeals to the human imagination; it speaks to dimensions of human experience that are included within what F. C. S. Northrop once called 'the aesthetic component' which Western intellectualism has so often overlooked or minimized by its stress on the 'rational component'. Furthermore, a symbol differs from a sign in that it establishes, however vaguely, a relationship between the person who sees it and uses it and whatever may be the reality to which it points. Paul Tillich helpfully made this point when he insisted that somehow a 'symbol participates in what is symbolized', whereas a sign (say a red or green traffic light) serves only utilitarian purposes and is merely both arbitrarily chosen and accepted by those who find it useful.

Mention of Tillich brings me to emphasize his argument that all speech, like all other representation or expression, about the aspects, areas or dimensions in our existence that are concerned with stressing the value, meaning, or significance and worth of life, is of a symbolic nature. At an earlier stage in his thinking, Tillich believed that in religious discourse the one literal statement was about 'being itself', while all else was of a symbolic nature; but I well remember the meeting of the American Theological Society in the late nineteen-forties (I happened to be president of the society and was in the chair at the session), when under considerable criticism and facing strong pressure from his fellow members of the society, Tillich conceded that even talk about 'being itself' was symbolic in quality. And in the preface to the second volume of his *Systematic Theology*, published some years later, he not only confirmed this change of mind but put considerable stress upon it, thereby giving his 'system' a consistency which previously it had lacked. *All* that we say about 'ultimate concern' – about the basic ground for the significance of human existence – is necessarily said in such a pictorial way. We may recall that somewhere in his writings G. K. Chesterton, English literary man of the earlier part of this century, remarked that 'we should not believe in anything that can't be told in "painted pictures" '. He was making exactly the same insistence as Tillich – that belief in the sense of commitment to, engagement in, and profound discernment of the grounding for our awareness of worth or value is an imaginative and hence a poetic venture.

I believe that the word 'model' can contain all this. It is not only a matter of intellectual acceptance; it is also, and even more deeply, a matter of emotional response. And as I have urged, a model becomes for us the focus of our thinking, feeling, and willing; it serves as an organizing centre for all that we do and think we are. Above all, it enables us to enter into kinds of experience that apart from it would not be open to our sharing. Hence, and in all these respects, it is in my view the most appropriate term to use when we are speaking of conceptions of God, who (almost by definition) is the guarantor of such significance and value or worth as basic to human existence. I need not labour the last point, however, since this has already been admirably argued by Professor Schubert Ogden in the opening essay of his *The Reality of God* (SCM Press and Harper and Row 1967).

Models are not created *ad hoc* by this or that individual. This is certainly the case when they are all-encompassing and speak most deeply to the human spirit. They have a communal aspect; they are shared with others and they have come to exist through a long period of preparation and development. There is a real continuity with the past in their coming to be accepted, while at the same time they have a certain genuine novelty since they are not exactly identical with what has gone before to make their emergence possible. As Kuhn and Barbour have recently demonstrated, even scientific models are not merely 'bolts from the blue'. A whole series of observations, various earlier intimations, and a sense of continuity with past experience have had their part in the suggestion of, and consequent acceptance of, the new model; and it receives general consent from the scientific community because it proves itself useful in illuminating what was hitherto known, while it also makes possible new experimental work which is confirmatory of its validity.

That is to say, the model *works*; it satisfactorily passes what might be called the pragmatic test. But it does more than that. It does not entirely contradict earlier models but rather corrects them and puts them in the proper perspective. It also opens up a whole range of new possibilities and opportunities for the future, which otherwise would not be available since previous models did not allow for the appearance of specific novelty. In other words, the model is seen as 'important'. I am using here one of Whitehead's terms, by which he wished to point to the value which this or that given particular event is recognized as possessing and which is thus integral to it. Furthermore, that which is thus seen to be important has what Whitehead styled 'consequences': it brings about results which themselves are also important.

This importance, seen in a given instance, varies from point to point. While all events have some measure of importance, in that they disclose something of what is going on in the world, some events have a special, even a decisive, importance. They are more satisfactory in their capacity to bring to a focus what has gone before; they are also more adequate in the present moment of understanding, experimentation, or observation; finally, they have an unusual way of suggesting *new* understanding, experimentation, and observation. The world is not a dull uniformitarian affair; on the contrary, it is marked by great variety, by what might well be called 'ups and downs' of meaning and of 'revealed' significance.

What has been said up to this point is peculiarly relevant when we turn to religious models, more especially the model which we use for that reality we call God. The way in which we picture deity, our conception of God (which we now see is associated with enormous imaginative and emotional content), our symbolic representation of the divine – that is, the model of God which we feel to be both possible and desirable in the light of our knowledge, experience, observation, our religious living, and our experimental procedure – provides for us an organizing centre, a focus for thought and act. Without some such model, we should have no opportunity to give a genuine grounding for the sense of life's significance and should be tossed to and fro, as it were without rudder, upon the sea of circumstance.

Within any given religious tradition, it seems to me, there are several requirements for a model which is to be acceptable and helpful. First of all, the model must be able to stand up to the knowledge which comes to us from the many and varied fields of human study and observation; it cannot be in flagrant contradiction of the best that we know from science and the other enterprises in which men and women engage in order to learn the truth about how things go in the world. Second, it must be imaginatively grasped, not merely accepted as an intellectually valid idea or notion, nor taken as a matter of theoretical speculation and as the logical conclusion of an argument. Thirdly, it must be engaging of the total personality of those who accept it, so that it serves them both as 'master-light' of their seeing and also as a means of empowering and strengthening, renewing and enabling them in their response to the vicissitudes of life.

All this; and something else, too. Any model which can be accepted and found valuable must have what I have called earlier a communal aspect. The very idea of tradition implies this. I have urged that nobody can manufacture, *de novo* and 'out of the whole cloth', a model which will appeal profoundly to the human spirit. To say that is also to say that the model must have some historical validation. Does it come to us, somehow or other, from the rich past of the tradition which we inherit? Is it somehow rooted in that tradition, of which it helps to make sense and which itself gives the model some degree of enduring significance? Is its very novelty not the sheer negation of earlier thought and experience, but rather the bringing to a climactic or focal point what has gone before, correcting that prior way of picturing deity but yet in continuity with that way? If the model we now propose can fulfil such requirements, it will prove attractive, even compelling; and it will thus prove itself, not because it is 'brand-new' but because it speaks to the depths in human experience and not only to the ever-present desire to see some new thing.

Of course there will be imprecision, there will be some 'rough edges'. But the fact is that, despite the Cartesian assertion that truth lies in 'clear and distinct ideas', the genuinely true is much more a matter of some vivid insight, rich and highly persuasive, which shades out into peripheral areas where there are nuances of greater or less intensity. So Whitehead urged; and I for one am sure that he was speaking for each of us when we consider our own awareness of what we like to call 'the truth'. Thus it is not necessary that our model shall completely and fully give us all the answers to all the questions we might feel impelled to ask. There will be a certain mystery here. We might even put it in this fashion: the chosen model should provide a clue to *meaning* in the midst of *mystery*. The circumambient mystery cannot be denied, but neither can the meaning which is spoken to us through the model.

In the next chapter we shall look at the model for God which in most Western theistic discussion has hitherto been taken for granted and which is enshrined in the theologies which we have inherited, be they 'Catholic' or 'Reformed'. We shall then go on to consider how that model has collapsed for vast numbers of our contemporaries, sometimes with a violent impact upon their experience although often enough with a more gradual dimming of its impression upon them. This will prepare us to look at another, or what I have called a new model – a model which, in my conviction, can meet the required tests and which above all can provide an organizing centre for the lives of men and women in our own day, illumination of their deepest human experience, and a genuine guarantee of the reality and validity of their sense that human existence indeed does have significance or worth and is not 'a tale told by an idiot, full of sound and fury, signifying nothing'.

2

The Old Model: 'Classical Theism'

It is easy enough to caricature the conventional model of God. We can speak of the old man in the sky, with full white beard and a severe frown on his face, whose eye somehow is supposed to be on each of us every moment of the time. Or we can speak of a stern monarch sitting on his throne, with hosts of heavenly beings prostrate before him, singing his praises in their endless alleluia. Again, we can speak of a judge, omniscient and intolerant, who with the open book of all human acts before him is prepared to hand out sentence: some of those on trial will go via purgatory to heaven, where they will presumably be rewarded for their goodness; most will go to hell, where they will endure unending torture as the due recompense for their wickedness in this life. Or if we are of a more liberal turn of mind, we can speak of a benign, fatherly figure who looks upon all his creatures as somewhat irresponsible children, but who yet regards them with considerable affection and is prepared to overlook the silliness which has led them to do unpleasing things.

All these caricatures, it may be noted, are in the masculine form. God is obviously the super-male; he may be tyrannical, patriarchal, judgmental, or benign but he is always modelled after the masculine and never after the feminine pattern. Of course, now and again, a bit of femininity may creep in: 'Can a Mother's tender care. . .?' asks one of the familiar hymns. So possibly there is a bit of tenderness about this predominantly male deity.

The descriptions just given are obviously anthropomorphic caricatures, fashioned in one way or another after the human likeness.

But there are others, too. Our list of caricatures, if it is to be adequate to the facts, must also include an unmoved mover, who despite the apparently personal character which such a phrase implies is much more like an abstract motionless impulsion exercised on others so that *they* will be impelled to act. It must include 'Being', subsisting from and of itself, in no way dependent upon anything not itself, and hence self-existent and self-contained. Although it may be said that in some odd fashion such 'Being' may produce or create other lesser and dependent 'beings', none makes an essential contribution to their producer or creator but exists only in utter dependence upon it or him. And there are other pictures as well, such as an unbending moral will which is often enough given a personal quality, but is always unyielding and inexorable in attitude.

Now, as I have urged, these are all of them caricatures. But as is frequently the case with caricatures, they point to something very real. They are pictures which are unpleasant or pleasant. Of course they do not correspond exactly to any theologically respectable definition of what conventional theologians have meant when they used the word 'God'. This must be granted; yet, despite the complaints of conservatively-minded religious people, above all theologians, who say that at no time and in no place in the history of Christian thought have any such models been regarded as exhaustive or even as true; despite protests that nobody has ever really believed that God was like any of them – the fact remains that the impression which has been given is not misrepresented by such caricatures.

We are told that in Victorian times some children's bedrooms had in them a painting showing a large eye, full-orbed and severe, which seemed to the young people to be staring at them continually, day and night. The title given that painting, it is said, was the phrase from St Augustine, 'Thou God seest me'. It is no wonder that children who saw such a painting every night tended to look upon God as a tyrant who spied out their every act and doubtless could read even their secret thoughts.

There was also in many minds a picture of God as what I can describe best as a cosmic manipulator. He had started things off, and to a good beginning; but somehow those created things went wrong. Then he would have to be called in to make the necessary adjustments. As a matter of fact, this is no total parody. Isaac Newton actually *did* believe that the God who created the world was obliged from time to time to intrude into that world so that the planets might proceed properly in their orbits – in fact, so that the Newtonian mechanically-conceived universe might be kept in order. In less sophisticated circles, God was conceived as in effect quite regularly 'tinkering', as we might put it, with the world. Every now and again he would do what one of the characters in the black play *Green Pastures* called 'pass a miracle', not necessarily because of some whim that suggested this as a good idea, but more often because the situation had so much got out of hand that only an intrusion from outside could repair the damage. In one such picture God was also required as the explanation to cover gaps in our scientific knowledge or observation. For example, since nobody had synthesized living matter out of inanimate matter, God was introduced as the reason for this change and so he served a useful purpose by bridging over *lacunae* which had been left without a natural linkage with previous causation.

Finally, in the specifically religious sphere, God was said to have organized what one writer of not so long ago, C. S. Lewis, was prepared to call a divine 'rescue expedition' to save men and women from their wrong doing and speaking and thinking. Others seemed to believe that in answer to prayer, more particularly if large numbers of people engaged in it, God could be persuaded to act, even to interfere, in the realm of nature and in human affairs. Thus he was invoked to avert a tidal wave, to cure an illness otherwise beyond recovery, to provide money for good people who needed it, to support a business enterprise, even to become the ally of a nation at war. A contemporary popular American preacher carried these ideas to an outlandish limit by proclaiming that those who properly believed in God would be successful in their financial dealings, win friends, and achieve high position in human society.

I have already admitted, indeed insisted, that none of these caricatures has ever been taught in exactly those ways by responsible thinkers in the Christian theological tradition. But as I have also said, the caricatures are sufficiently apt to make it necessary to examine exactly what has been happening in the world of Christian theology during the past centuries. How does it come about that such incredible and unbelievable pictures have got into the minds of multitudes of men and women?

We are given a partial clue in some words of Whitehead, found in his book *Modes of Thought* (The Free Press 1938, p. 49). Whitehead wrote,

When the religious thought of the ancient world from Mesopotamia to Palestine, and from Palestine to Egypt, required terms to express that ultimate unity of direction in the universe, upon which all order depends, and which gives meaning to importance, they could find no better way to express themselves than by borrowing the characteristics of the touchy, vain, imperious tyrants who ruled the empires of the world. In the origin of civilized societies, gods are like dictators. Our modern rituals still retain this taint.

Whitehead adds, in words that will be helpful to us in our suggestions about a different model from these,

> The most emphatic repudiations of this archaic notion are to be found scattered in the doctrines of Buddhism and in the Christian Gospels.

Here we have an insight into the reason for the modelling of God after what the same writer styled 'imperial Caesar'. But there were other ingredients, more particularly as Christian thinkers in the early days of the church came to articulate more precisely their doctrine of God. For one thing, there was the influence of certain aspects of Greek philosophy. This kind of thinking, very prevalent in religious-minded circles of the ancient world, identified perfection with absolute changelessness. In terms of their way of thinking there was some point in this identification. For, if any sort of change could be predicated, that meant either change for the better, which was unthinkable if deity was indeed perfect, or change for the worse, which was equally unthinkable since God could never be less than complete and whole and could never be susceptible to anything that was not entirely good.

Or once again, since our experience and observation plainly demonstrated that in the world where we live, and with ourselves in that world, there was contingency and hence mutability, pain and suffering, all manner of evil, any conception of God which asserted deity to be perfect must include precisely the opposite of those creaturely facts and experiences. Hence God must be immutable, in no sense possessed of contingency, without the capacity to experience or share in pain or suffering. His goodness must be the exact contrary of these, because these were phenomena in a world where evil was to be seen. If God were like this, he must be above all temporal succession; he must be eternal in the sense that he possessed at once whatever had occurred temporally, whatever was now occurring in the realm of historical happening, and whatever was going to take place in such a realm. He must know simultaneously and without any successiveness, all the past, present, and future. At the same time he was unaffected and uninfluenced by what takes place in the entirely dependent creation which he had brought into being – usually thought to have taken place at some specific moment in the distant past. Nothing could make a contribution to him; or better to 'it', since such a picture of God as *esse a se subsistens* or *ens realissimum*, to use phrases from the Middle Ages and from eighteenth century theologians, requires the neuter gender and has to do with what one of our present-day thinkers has called 'being *itself*' as an appropriate definition of deity.

There was the model of 'imperial Caesar'; there was the model of philosophical 'self-existence'. And there was also the model derived from long Jewish tradition. Here we must be careful lest we do injustice to that tradition, which had many facets and great variety in its thinking about the one whom the Jews called Jahweh – God as disclosed to them, so they thought, in their historical experience as a people who felt themselves uniquely 'chosen' to be his servants. The slow development of Jewish thought about God, in the response made by that ancient Semitic people to their experience during many centuries, is portrayed for us in the Old Testament. But the early Christian theologians did not have our advantage in understanding the variety of views developed in that long period and above all in recognizing that the Old Testament picture is not all 'of a piece'. On the contrary, they took it as it stood, so to say; and for them one of the dominant motifs, perhaps even *the* dominant motif, was God in his moral demands. This God was utterly righteous; and his righteous will was revealed both in the 'commandments' which he had given to Moses on Mount Sinai and also in the punishments which he was thought to mete out to those who refused to obey him. He was a stern, unbending moral lord.

There were other and gentler, more gracious aspects and elements in the Jewish tradition, to be sure. But by and large these do not seem to have played so large a role in the development of later ideas of deity such as the Christian theologians in question undertook. They did not know, as we do (and a later chapter will emphasize the point now being made), that the history of Hebrew religion moves forward from what scholars style 'primitive Yahwism', with God envisaged as sheer coercive power manifested in storm and earthquake and battle, to the Mosaic grasp of God's power as always exercised for justice – as 'the Power that makes for righteousness', in Matthew Arnold's admirable phrase; and beyond that, through much in the prophetic tradition, notably in Hosea, parts of Isaiah, and Jeremiah as found in the Old Testament, to stress what the Jews called the divine *chesed*, best translated as God's 'faithful loving-mercy', whose operation in human affairs had for its goal the establishment among his people of *shalom* or abundant and full human existence, in a social context and with increasing awareness of the divine concern for the non-Jewish peoples, the *goyim*, or 'gentiles'. Had such a movement been properly understood by early theologians – and there were *some* of them who glimpsed it and who used the Old Testament more or less in the fashion which that development would demand, but they were relatively few and some of them, like Origen, were regarded as heretics – the excessive emphasis upon God's moral nature, in a direction which amounted to moral dictatorship with a whole calculus of rewards and punishments included in the picture, might have been avoided. Alas, this was not the case. So we have as a third ingredient in the conventional model of God what can only be called (with Whitehead) 'ruthless moralism'.

In such a model of God, it is inevitable that he will be seen as one who is so much the ordering reality that anything and everything that happens in the world, for good or for evil, is his responsibility. Either he wills it directly or he 'permits' it to occur when things could have been otherwise – and this permission is supposed to be given with a view to some end which appears desirable to him. What is more, the combination of despotic rule, metaphysical unchangeableness or immutability, and moral demand brings with it the insistence that nothing in the creation can make any contribution to, or in any way affect or influence or alter, the divine being. Obviously the world is related to God as its creator; it is totally dependent upon him both for its existence and for its continuance; the relationship is in that respect a *real* one. But God is related to the world in only one way: in a logical mode, since he *is* its creator and preserver. He can receive nothing from that world, since already, in his sheer perfection, he already *has* everything and *is* everything.

But what of the specific Christian affirmation of the disclosure of God in Jesus Christ? Certainly, it will be said – and rightly – that the Christian theological tradition from its earliest days gave a central place to the figure of Jesus Christ. Did not acceptance of that central place necessarily require very serious modification of the picture of God as dictator, umoved mover, and moral governor? The New Testament says that 'God is Love'; and it affirms that we know this, not as a speculation or a theory, but because 'God loved us and sent his Son that we might live through him.' So I John puts it; so all Christians have believed. Why did not that proclamation, taken as central in faith as men and women respond to what is exhibited and enacted in Jesus Christ, receive such an emphasis that whatever was said about the divine rule, the divine creativity, and the divine moral concern, would then be said with a difference?

This question is difficult to answer. In certain respects the event of Christ did make a difference; and a very important difference, too. But in other respects it seems to have made very little difference. I suggest that the reason for this ambiguity is found in the distinction between what might be called 'working religion' and 'theological consideration'. We might say that religious experience concerned itself more with the disclosure of God as related in love to his children, while theological interest was much more directed to producing a doctrinal system that was coherent and philosophically adequate – always assuming, of course, that such coherence and adequacy were then understood in terms of the world-view and general metaphysical position taken for granted in the ancient world in which the theology was being developed.

Perhaps one way of putting this would be by recognizing that the definition of God, in his very essence, was derived from philosophy as it was commonly accepted, and then was qualified religiously and (as we may say) in an adjectival fashion by what was revealed in Jesus Christ. What is God? He is prime substance, being itself, unmoved mover, changeless perfection. He is also moral governor and ruler of the world – here cultural influence and a too uncritical reading of the Old Testament played the dominant role. But that absolute reality, moral governor, worshipful by all his creation, is also taken to be loving. The noun is the former set of ideas; the adjective is the latter. Unhappily, however, the adjective did not always or often receive the emphasis which it would have received if the experiential religious fact had been given primacy.

In this connection, I may remark that it has often seemed to me, as I read the writings of some of the greatest theologians in Christian history – often Origen, certainly St Augustine, St Thomas Aquinas, Martin Luther, and John Calvin – that I am meeting in each of them two different personalities. On the one hand, there is the man with a deep faith in God, often a vigorous insistence on his loving care and his gracious concern with the creation, and with a feeling of a personal relationship which is enjoyed between a prevenient Lover and a creaturely lover-in-the-making who seeks to respond to that prevenience. This is prominent and deeply moving. On the other hand, there is a theological position which seems quite different, with its insistence on absoluteness, unrelatedness, unchangeableness, and impassibility or inability to share in the world's anguish. Sometimes an effort is made to bring these two into some sort of unity. But, by and large, the unity which is achieved tends to lay its major emphasis on the more metaphysical side or to put the stress on the moral demands. Of course the assertion of God's love is never denied, but it is given a secondary (or adjectival) place.

It is illuminating in this respect to study St Augustine, for example. He has sometimes been called 'the doctor of the divine Love'; and that is indeed the case when we read many of his sermons, or his outpouring of personal experience in *The Confessions*, or other comments scattered through his many books. Yet when we come to his considered theological affirmations about God, we find that he is much more a platonizing theologian who (alas) does not stress those parts of Plato (which perhaps he did not know, or know well) where persuasion rather than coercion is central.

Or take Aquinas. Here his sermons, along with his *Explicationes* of the Creed as well as his liturgical creations like the Corpus Christi office, speak in terms of the loving father of Jesus Christ who had disclosed himself to his children and acted to bring them to himself as they responded in faith to that Jesus. But elsewhere, when St Thomas is writing his systematic exposition of Christian theology in the *Summa Theologica*, it is Aristotelianism, with its unmoved mover, the thinker thinking his thoughts, unrelated perfection, and the like which become the points of reference, however many biblical texts are adduced. Indeed, it might be said that even in the *Summa* itself this contradiction or at least inconsistency may be seen. This is shown when we notice that in his responses to objections, St Thomas makes much of the distinctions between possible meanings of terms – *distinguo*, he says over and over again. Often enough those distinctions might be described as between the religious understanding in faith, on the one hand, and the more philosophical ideas which are advanced, on the other.

Or to turn to a great Reformation theologian, the philosophical background of Luther is less obvious, although it is present in the voluntarism which Luther had learned from Gabriel Biel's late medieval scholasticism. But we find a sharp contrast between God as known in his *opus alienum*, the Old Testament severity and moral intransigence, and God in his *opus proprium*, where he is shown as the 'gracious God' whose nature is altogether Love for his creation and above all for his bewildered, erring and unhappy human children.

In their very useful book *Process Theology: An Introductory Exposition* (Westminster Press 1976), John Cobb and David Griffin note five ingredients in this conventional 'classical' model of God (pp. 8–10): (1) cosmic moralist; (2) unchanging and passionless being; (3) controlling power; (4) sanctioner and defender of the *status quo*; (5) dominant male. I have touched on most of these in this chapter. I should wish to add to my own discussion something more of their emphasis on the way in which, in the older model, God has been regarded as primarily the firm supporter of things as they are: the *status quo*. For those who take this view, all 'liberation theology' is naturally an anathema. Likewise, those who identify 'old time religion' with the continuation of the old model must find that new or different ways of thinking are a denial of what they take the Christian doctrine of God to be. I shall not dwell on this, however. Nor shall I do more than apologize for the way in which, now and again, I myself may have seemed in this book to speak of God as masculine by use of the personal pronoun 'he'. I hope that the reader will understand that this has been for convenience' sake only; and that I am quite prepared to substitute what grammatically seems to me a difficult word 's/he' for God, as so many nowadays prefer. In any event, God is *not* male; the father image, which in later chapters will be stressed, must be supplemented by the mother image – which, by the way, is not really modern, since (in the Middle Ages and even earlier) God and Jesus, too, were now and again called 'mother' as we notice in Julian of Norwich's *Shewings*.

The basic problem with the older model, religiously speaking – and there are other problems as well, to which we shall turn in the next chapter – is to be seen in the failure to make absolutely and not nominally central, and to establish as the fundamental criterion for all Christian theological discourse, the affirmation that God *is* Love. God is the 'pure unbounded love' of which Charles Wesley's hymn speaks, in its self-disclosure in the event of Jesus Christ and the experientially validated witness to him in the Christian fellowship. Perhaps nowhere has this basic Christian insight been stated more beautifully than in the very early *Epistle to Diognetus*, with some words from which I end this chapter and which will provide also an introduction to a new model for God, with which we shall directly concern ourselves in the fourth chapter:

Did God send him, as a human mind might assume, to rule by tyranny, fear, or terror? Far from it! He sent him out of kindness and gentleness, like a King sending his Son who is himself a king. He sent him as God; he sent him as man to men. He willed to save men by persuasion, not by compulsion, for compulsion is not God's way of working. In sending him God called men. He sent him in love, not in judgment. No man has ever seen God nor made God known, but he has manifested himself; and he has manifested himself to faith, by which alone it has been possible for us to see God. For God showed himself to be a true friend of man. O, the overflowing kindness of God towards men! God did not hate us, nor drive us away, nor bear us ill-will . . . Think then how you will love him, who first loved you so.

3

The Breakdown of the Old Model: 'The Death of God'

What I have called the old or conventional model of God, omnipotent and absolute, unrelated and immutable, impassible and self-contained, moral dictator and imperial ruler, unquestionably continues to make some sort of sense to millions of men and women in the Western world. With this eternal self-sufficiency of God, so conceived, God is somehow paradoxically associated as a loving and concerned parent, who provides for and looks after his human children, although he does this (to a considerable extent) by interfering on their behalf and adjusting the ways of the world so that they can live in relative security and have a promise of heavenly bliss after this life. The two emphases do not fit together very readily; and therefore the ingenuity of theologians is exercised in attempting to work out as consistent and coherent a pattern as possible. In the end, however, there is a great mystery – and here it is mystery, not in the proper sense of the incapacity of the human mind to fathom the depths of the divine life and love, but much more in the sense of a tragic recognition that ideas of absolute omnipotence and entire self-sufficiency do not go very well with ideas of profound caring and generous love.

Nevertheless, as I have said, vast numbers of people are still prepared to continue with this ill-fitting union, and to accept the model which traditional theology offers for their interpretation of religious understanding and for the explanation of the sense of 'comradeship and refreshment' (to use a phrase of Whitehead's, to which I shall return in another chapter) which a deeply-believed religious attitude can and often does make available. Indeed we can say that in many quarters, where newer notions and more modern knowledge seem to threaten men and women, there has been a considerable return to the old model. It appears to provide security; and it has been the traditional background against which vitalizing faith has been taken to be a significant reality, giving a context for the feeling of life's significance and worth. This is the reason that we are seeing an astonishing recrudescence of conservative religion and the extraordinary appeal which fundamentalist sects seem able to make in an age in which their pretensions to credibility and intellectual respectability are patently false.

But it must also be noted that while there is this continuing acceptance of the old model in some quarters, at the same time among other people there is an increasing rejection both of that model and of the kind of religion which it entails. The 'secularization' of human existence goes on with undiminished force and, even among those who still accept in their religious moments the older set of beliefs, there is a practical secularity in their ordinary day-by-day living. Yet, in the experience of vast numbers of men and women who do not live bifurcated lives, there is an outright 'no' to the old model. For millions of people today, especially in the more sophisticated countries of Europe, America and the Antipodes, 'God' in the model described in the last chapter is dead.

A few years ago, in the United States and Britain, and to some extent elsewhere, there was much talk of 'the death of God'. The movement called by this name is said no longer to be much in evidence; probably that is true enough, insofar as public attention and concern are in view. Its best-known exponents do not seem to be much heard of, nowadays; we have moved on to other matters. But it is my experience that what those exponents were saying was an expression of what an untold number of people still do think, even if they are not able to articulate their thought in such a clear and unmistakeable fashion.

During the height of the discussion of 'the death of God', I ventured to urge in several articles in theological and religious journals that the real point was not that somehow or other 'God had died', but rather that certain notions of God – those commonly identified with one aspect or another of the old model – had died on the writers who popularized the phrase about God's 'death'. The model to which these men had given their assent in their earlier years was no longer a workable model for them to accept. And since they had simply identified that model with the divine reality itself, they were compelled to speak as they did. They had not known any other model, nor did they feel required to seek for one which would lack the several characteristics which were no longer viable in their experience. For this they could hardly be blamed, since the previous post-War II religious and theological revival in which they had been caught up had all too often presupposed just such a model; indeed the model had been reasserted with vigour and enthusiasm by many 'neo-orthodox' and 'biblical' theologians. If that model would no longer serve, if it was defective or absurd in many respects, the reaction could follow, and did follow, that there was no sense in talking about God at all. That model was the *one* model for God; the theologians and philosophers who talked in terms of other models – and of course there were such people – were not believed to be talking about God in the manner in which Christian thought had always conceived him. So it appeared that the honest thing to do was to deny the old model, a denial which was entirely proper and correct; but with that denial also to deny God himself, which was both unnecessary and thoughtless.

I think that we may say that the old model has broken down in a number of important respects. At the same time, I am convinced that this does not for a moment mean that God can no longer be thought real, nor that his existence can no longer be maintained by men and women of intellectual integrity. On the contrary, I urge that the old model has broken down because it was, and is, incredible and impossible both in itself and in its consequences for theology. And I further urge that this break-down is, so to say, an invitation to responsible thinkers to suggest a new model which can stand up to criticism, meet the objections which quite rightly were made to the old one, and offer to men and women in our own day a viable way of understanding God and his action in the world.

Why then did the old model collapse for so many people in so many places? Five reasons may be suggested. I shall list them and then discuss them. These reasons have a certain over-lap; but the listing which I shall give and then consider provides a convenient way of seeing the matter.

Here, then, is my list: (1) philosophical problems which the old model presented; (2) a view of divine transcendence which made deity appear irrelevant to human experience; (3) the problem of language used about deity; (4) scientific knowledge which ruled out finally any conception of 'gaps' to be filled by God; (5) the old model's apparent denial, or at least its minimizing, of human integrity, freedom, decision, and accountability or responsibility. I realize, of course, that a discussion of the first (philosophical) topic will of necessity be somewhat academic; for this I ask pardon of my readers, promising that the four other points can be and will be considered in a much simpler and more direct fashion.

1. In my student days in the twenties and thirties, the prevalent philosophy, so far at least as English-speaking religious circles were concerned, was idealism or (as it has been better named) 'mentalism'. The materialistic outlook which had been significant in the nineteenth century, and especially towards the close of that period, had brought about a reaction from the more influential empiricism of an earlier age. Spiritual realities were taken to be supreme and the world of matter was derivative from the realm of the Spirit. Let me speak about this from my own days in Oxford. There the outstanding exponent of such idealism was C. C. J. Webb, undoubtedly a great thinker and certainly a devout Christian believer. Before him there had been such men as T. H. Green, and contemporary with him was Hastings Rashdall, to name but one influential Oxford don, who later became Dean of Carlisle. 'Personalistic idealism' was the mode. We find this expressed in theologians like the then important Charles Gore and in the earlier writings of A. E. Taylor. In North America, too, the idealistic school had a remarkable appeal to the religious world.

God was either Absolute Spirit or (as with such English metaphysicians as F. H. Bradley) was the highest theological conception, under such Absolute Spirit, that we could entertain if 'Spirit was reality' and God was not to be pantheistically identified – perhaps monistically would be a better adverb here – with the absolute. While not many theologians were followers of Hegel and his German school of absolute idealism, there can be little doubt that his influence was significant. In Oxford only a few men, like Robin Collingwood, stood out against this, but even they were idealists of a sort. In Cambridge things were slightly different, yet men like MacTaggart, Sorley, and their disciples were regarded in religious circles as on the side of the angels. Of course there were others, F. R. Tennant and James Ward, for example, who could not entirely be fitted into the idealistic pattern. So also at Oxford the 'humanist' F. C. S. Schiller, whose humanism was in fact a variety of pragmatism, did not quite fit. In Scotland the influence of A. S. Pringle-Pattison was strong and his idealism, combined with the native Scots emphasis on moral principles, produced still another variety of idealism – in this instance what might also be styled 'personal idealism', although that term had been used differently by the Oxford dons who contributed to the symposium which bore that title and to the religious philosophy found in such apologetic writing as the other symposium *Contentio Veritatis*.

My introduction to philosophy had been through lectures from
Archibald Allan Bowman, a Scotsman who was at the time teaching
philosophy at Princeton University. He was a somewhat eclectic
thinker who did not quite fit fully into the idealistic camp; yet there
were strong elements of such idealism in his lectures. Dr John Grier
Hibben, President of Princeton, had been a professor before he
became an administrator; and I recall vividly his own semi-Hegeli-
anism, largely derived from the so-called 'St Louis Hegelian school'
and influenced also by Josiah Royce and his Harvard variety of
philosophical idealism.

At the same time, however, there were younger thinkers both in
Britain and North America, as well as in Europe and in Australia,
who were working along other lines. They were more empirical,
pragmatic, and realist in their outlook. Some of them had studied
under or felt the strong influence of that many-sided genius William
James, even if they did not subscribe totally to his radical empiricism.
Others were affected by the thought of Henri Bergson, with his
emphasis on creativity and life. Sooner rather than later, then, the
school of philosophical idealism seemed to lose its appeal. Even in
religious circles there was a turn away from it, more particularly in
the United States, to other and newer views. But it is interesting that
when Alfred North Whitehead went to Harvard University in the
1920s, he was not regarded as having any novel contribution to
make. He was enormously respected, but for his work in the
philosophy of science rather than for any hints of a metaphysical
position which was to be quite different from that popular in those
days, either at Harvard or elsewhere.

I came to an appreciation of Whitehead (and Hartshorne, too)
after a period during which I had been much impressed by the neo-
Thomism of Jacques Maritain and Etienne Gilson. The Oxford
idealism, in which I had been nurtured (so to say), would no longer
serve me precisely because of what I have often called its grandiose
omnicompetence. It seemed to know altogether too much about
heaven and earth and all things between those two. The neo-Thomism
which was then dominant in thoughtful Roman Catholic circles was
also omnicompetent; but it had the virtue of beginning down on earth
and its theory of knowledge was realistic rather than almost entirely
'mental'. Nor was I alone in this interest in the insight, if not the
precise details, of the neo-scholastic revival. The varieties of realism
(which were prevalent at the time in many philosophical circles,
especially in the United States) were in reaction against the earlier
idealism, and were concerned to stress an approach to human
knowledge which was not up in the clouds, but based upon the

concrete facts of human experience in the world which we knew. A qualified realism, either using the basic neo-Thomist insight or some similar view, was also to be found in the writing of Baron Friedrich von Hügel, the distinguished Austrian-English religious philosopher of the first few decades of the century, who at this time was one of my favourite thinkers in the Catholic tradition.

But as with Oxford idealism, so also with the neo-Thomist philosophy of the time. If it was not so pretentious in its claims to knowledge and if it was more modest because of its acceptance of the sense of mystery upon which St Thomas himself had been so insistent, it was still much too omnicompetent – or so I thought. The narrow Thomism of the Roman Curia and ultra-conservative theologians was of that type. But, fortunately, many Roman Catholic thinkers (e.g. Karl Rahner) who were in that general Thomist tradition were moving increasingly, if cautiously, in the direction of what was called transcendental Thomism; this was in fact a combination of many neo-Thomist insights with the existentialist ideas of Heidegger and others, as well as open, in many cases, to the phenomenological thinking of Husserl. To me it seemed to be a verbal attempt to save the appearances of neo-Thomist philosophy itself. In consequence – and with many other criticisms which could be made – the whole neo-Thomist philosophical approach to the belief in God seemed in my view also to be breaking down for many thinkers in the Catholic tradition. What was to take its place? For some in the Roman Catholic Church, perhaps for many more than was known, it was and continues to be the Whiteheadian 'vision of reality' which made its appeal. Increasingly this has been obviously the case in the United States and Latin America, and more recently on the continent of Europe as well.

This is not the place to continue with the story nor to comment further on the revised- or neo-Thomism which prevailed for a time in more Catholic circles. Suffice it to say that in the thirties and forties the whole philosophical climate changed. One strong school, to a considerable degree influenced by the Vienna Circle but also inheriting the empiricism of Hume from a much earlier British period, came to be known as linguistic philosophy. For this school, *all* metaphysical talk seemed to be 'nonsense'. In a later chapter I shall have something to say about language and more particularly about what John Macquarrie has well called 'God-talk'. For the moment I wish only to say that the breakdown, in many quarters, of philosophical idealism as well as Thomistic 'realism' had much to do with altering what in religious circles could be assumed as a suitable context for theological work. Let me put this briefly and personally. It was in the late thirties and early forties that I began (as I have said) to be suspicious of the grandiose, omnicompetent, all-explanatory Oxford philosophical idealism in which I had been brought up. As I noted above, it seemed too pretentious; it knew altogether too much about the cosmos as a whole and about God in relation to the cosmos. It had a place for everything and it wished to keep everything in that place. So I had turned to the newer variety of Thomism as represented by Jacques Maritain. But considered as a whole, not least in its more optimistic view of things, it too lost its attraction. I believe that this has been true of many others. Even the efforts of Paul Tillich, with his Schelling type of philosophy, could not restore confidence in idealism or Thomism, however attractive might have been the existentialist analysis of experience with which he and others associated them.

2. In a more specifically religious sense, the earlier emphasis upon divine transcendence had been seriously qualified by the newer stress on divine immanence. Liberal theology in particular was important here. For that theology, God was not so much above the world as he was in it; there he could be found, in the world of human experience above all, but also in the realm of nature. For that theology, however, the world was a realm in which the more tragic, yet as we now see inescapable, negative aspects of life tended to be overlooked. Liberal theology collapsed precisely for this reason, once the affect of war, depression, and human suffering was felt seriously in the thirties and forties of the century. In conventional religious circles, on the other hand, the important matter was still transcendence. And when the neo-orthodox theology, under Karl Barth and Emil Brunner and their disciples on both sides of the Atlantic, reacted against immanentism and indeed against the earlier trends in philosophical theology generally, the divine transcendence became the dominant religious conviction, although it was interpreted in what was said to be a more strictly biblical sense. The divine sovereignty, the 'otherness' of deity, and the incapacity of human beings to find a way to God because there was a 'no passage' sign, were reasserted. The way from God to man became the only fashion in which we could know anything about God. Here was a revival of what was called Reformation theology, biblical theology, or revelational theology.

But at this point, the sharp criticism directed by both linguistic philosophers and neo-orthodox theologians against all human speculation concerning God, their denial of meaning to the Catholic doctrine of analogy, and their insistence that human sin was manifested, not only in emotion and will, but above all in pretensions to knowledge of deity (thereby conforming God to our own ideas, as it was said), began to have its consequences. Here we come to the third ingredient in my listing, which I shall mention more briefly.

3. The very arguments which linguistic philosophers and neo-orthodox theologians directed against natural theology or philosophy of religion, could equally well be applied to what the latter thinkers said about 'revealed' truth. Even when this was not looked at as propositions about deity but as the self-disclosure of God himself, it was open to drastic criticism. Paul van Buren in his book *The Secular Meaning of the Gospel* provides an interesting example here. He had begun as a fairly strict Barthian. But he began to read the English and American linguistic philosophers; and soon he saw that 'revelation'-talk about God could be analysed and criticized and questioned as to its possibility of verification and its reference to known data. He was honest enough to see that the theology of revelation could not stand up to such an appraisal. Hence he had to find a strictly human and historical reference for what that theology had said. The result was what he styled a 'secular' gospel, although he allowed for some dimension of human experience, above all in the search for freedom, which could provide an area for religious speech. More recently van Buren has again changed his mind and seems now to have returned to a quasi-Barthian position. Yet what he said in his famous book was revealing, since it confirmed the general suspicion that statements about deity needed at least very careful treatment and usage, not least when they were phrased in idealistic idiom and particularly when they entailed emphasis on revelation as the only source of knowledge about deity.

4. We come now to the scientific knowledge of our time. Science has become more humble than it was in the late nineteenth century. Talk about 'laws which never shall be broken' is less frequent; the quantum theory, the relativity principle, and in general the new physics have been important in shifting the claim from complete competence to that of adequate description. But that does not mean that science has any place for the 'gaps' where God was supposed to introduce himself to bring about novelties in the world. There was a continuity of process, so to say; and scientists still maintain that this is the case although they now admit the appearance of novelty.

But even more important, for our present purpose, is the enormous advance in technology in all areas – from medical discovery and treatment of illness all the way to biological engineering; and other sorts of engineering too.

The result has been that the world as science discloses it to us is not a world where divine causality can be introduced at point after point. It is not a world in which intrusions or interruptions of natural sequences are either expected or discovered. What is more, it has turned out to be a world in which Francis Bacon's adage about 'knowledge as power' is increasingly demonstrated as applicable to more and more fields of enquiry, with astonishing results that are sometimes beneficial and sometimes (alas) ambiguous if not detrimental, like use of atomic energy, nuclear research, and their consequences. I need not dwell on all this; it is obvious to most of us from our reading and from what we hear on radio and television. Even the less highly educated sections of the population are more and more aware of what has been going on; many people listen avidly to what is taken to be the latest deliverance of science obtained through experiment or observation. What it amounts to is an undermining of any support from experiment and observation for the old model of God as absolute controller, as occasional manipulator, or as necessarily to be introduced into any difficult situation as the solver of our problem. God, it would seem, is no longer needed, if by God we mean what the old model seemed to imply.

5. We have also witnessed a vigorous reaction to the apparent denial of human integrity, freedom, decision, and accountability or responsibility which for many seemed to follow from the older model. We are aware of the increasing secularization of life which all of us experience in our time. It is here, I believe, that we find the major reason for the collapse of the old model of God, at least so far as the general public is concerned.

As everyone knows, Dietrich Bonhoeffer wrote in one of his letters from prison during the Nazi regime in Germany that 'man has come of age'. This remark has been seriously misunderstood. But read in context, along with some of his other comments about 'religion' and 'religionless Christianity', it makes very good sense. What Bonhoeffer was asserting was not that human beings are entirely mature and in that sense fully 'of age'. Rather, he was getting at the profound truth that in our own day thoughtful men and women are more and more determined to accept responsibility, to be held accountable, to be treated with the respect due to their human integrity, and to have it recognized that they are possessed of a degree of genuine freedom and hence can and do make meaningful decisions about matters which concern them. They refuse to be treated as children who continually run to 'Daddy' when difficulties arise and who can always turn to him to put things right when they are going wrong. Today, people do not believe that they are servile slaves and they refuse to be treated as such.

Now this is a fact which even the most unobservant can see. It runs straight through human society. People are not willing to be shoved around or manipulated, if they can in any way and by any means avoid such treatment. They want to stand on their own feet; they would like always to be treated as those who have genuine human dignity.

To think and act in this fashion does not necessarily entail an irreligious attitude. One of the worst aspects of the old model for God was that by portraying him as an oriental despot it suggested, indeed required, that his human children should cringe before him in abject fear or, if not that, should regard themselves as totally incompetent and helpless creatures. As one of the Psalms puts it, they were 'worms and no men'. Percy Dearmer, an English parson of the earlier years of the century, used to criticize much hymnody because it took what he called (following the 'worm' image) 'a vermiform view of man'. If that sort of thing was found in hymns, it was also found in much of our traditional liturgical material and in many sermons. Now and again we still hear this denigration of humanity as a presumed incentive to greater belief in an omnipotent God.

But the day is long since past when any of this will 'go down' with most people. Even in conservative religious circles, for instance, liturgical revision has been carried on with a view to stressing a different understanding of ourselves, while the hymns now being written take a quite different line. In any event, the ordinary man or woman wishes to assert, and continually does assert, his or her dignity as a human, a sense of responsibility for what is done, and a readiness to face the consequences of the decisions which this or that person has made. This is not to say that people today have no sense of sin, as it is often argued. What it means is that sin is commonly understood in a manner quite different from that which the old model appeared to suggest. Human defection, distortion, and wrongness are seen nowadays more in injustice, hateful attitudes to others, hypocrisy, and the like, whether in personal relationships or in social affairs. Human beings do not think that they are perfect; but they do believe that they are men and women who matter and who can act significantly.

I recall one of the 'death of God' thinkers who was telling me how he came to his position. He had been brought up in a quite conservative religious denomination; he had decided upon the ministry and had then gone to a theological college which was neo-orthodox in outlook. He had accepted without question the stark Calvinism, suitably updated, which that theological school taught. Then, in his early ministry, he had seen social abuses, stark injustice, hateful human behaviour, and above all (in his case) the disintegration of the inner city. When he talked about such matters to others, speaking with a deeply troubled conscience and expecting from fellow-Christians a response which would entail concerted efforts to do what might be possible to better conditions, he was horrified to discover that he met with indifference – or what was worse, he said, with a continual 'harping on personal conversion as the solution for all these problems'. Perhaps he was irrational or extreme in the way in which he met this kind of response. But at least it was understandable that he began to ally himself with the non-religious, non-Christian, and often very secular agencies which shared his deep concern. He left his fellow-Christians to 'their own privatized religion', as he put it. In the end, he concluded that the God in whom he had believed – or, as I would prefer to say, the model of God which he had accepted – was irrelevant to the things that really mattered to him. That God was for him 'dead'; and so he gave up what he had taken to be his Christian faith, although he declared that he still 'took his stand with Jesus' in his love for and concern about his human brothers and sisters.

In an aggravated, but by no means untypical fashion, this honest and earnest clergyman represents what is the feeling of very many people. The old model of God, as one who cannot be affected by human activity and who in any event is so much self-contained that he does not participate in the world's anguish as in its joy, is of no use. There is no evidence that such a God does in fact continually intervene in the world's affairs to right that which is wrong. He appears to be primarily interested in the adoration he receives and the obedience he demands. He does not really count in ordinary life. He gets more and more remote from all that is of vital importance to men and women. 'Very well,' they say, 'let us forget about him.' Eventually he vanishes from sight and becomes nothing more than a remembered fantasy, superstitiously believed in at one time, but no longer worth attention. Indeed, for many he probably does not even 'exist'. But of course it is not God as the truly worshipful, ever-faithful source of refreshment and strength, who purposes new things done through the agency of created causes, who receives into his divine life whatever good is accomplished, and above all who joins his children in their struggle against what is evil. . .it is not *God himself* who has died. It is only an old and outmoded model of God, which has been shown to be incredible and useless and which some of us believe ought to be discarded to make place for what we dare to call a defensible and also genuinely Christian model.

4

A New Model: Whitehead's Proposal

In the first chapter, in which we discussed the place and function of models in human experience, it was argued that such models provide a focus and centre for the organization of what we know and understand. It was also argued that experience itself is so related with and conditioned by such models that it may be impossible for certain kinds of experience to be had if those models are incredible or absurd or highly irrelevant to those who hold them or think they should accept them. In this respect, a model, above all a model for the supreme reality (if there be such a reality), will open up the possibility of deeper understanding and more significant experience.

Nobody can doubt that many people have had, and that many still do have, a genuine experience of that reality through their acceptance of the old model for deity. This is because, at one time and under the conditions of that time, such a model made sense and did not contradict all the rest of their world of understanding. It was also because the old model did assert, or sought to assert as one element in it, truths which were meaningful and illuminating, above all in that it contained or included *some* affirmation about the love of God, his care for his human children, and his faithfulness to his purposes of goodness. An affirmation like that has always spoken with meaning to men and women by confirming their sense of life's significance and providing for them some guarantee of the worth of human action. The trouble was that this kind of affirmation was taken as *theologically* adjectival – although of course necessary for actual religious living – to the substantive portrayal of deity in terms of absoluteness, dictatorship or control, and moral intransigence. These substantive assertions were so dominant that they produced a sort of schizophrenic piety, of which perhaps Luther's anguishing feeling (already noted in this book) of the contradiction between God's *opus alienum* and his *opus proprium* may serve as a notable instance.

In this chapter I shall present a model for deity (initially proposed by Whitehead) in which what in the old model was taken to be adjectival is made 'substantive' – or better, as we shall urge in the sequel, is given ontological priority, but yet is seen as 'verbal', since God is envisaged as active and dynamic energy and not as belonging to the order of nouns or 'things'. Much that had been given first place and seen as substantive, now becomes adverbial to the basic or primary assertion. I have said adverbial because verbs are modified or qualified or given fuller meaning through the use of adverbs, while adjectives are used to qualify nouns – which is to say, 'things', whether these are considered divine or human.

But before I present a sketch of the new model, something must first be said about the kind of world to which this model is relevant. Any model must be related to, and must make sense in terms of, the world as it actually is seen to be. This was not the case with the old model; and as the years have gone by and new knowledge has been acquired thanks to science and analysis of human existence, the 'fit' has become less and less possible between that model for God and the world about which the model is supposed to be illuminating. What sort of world is it, then, in which most of us today think ourselves to be living?

The world, as we now know, is 'made up' of dynamic events. It is not composed of things which have simple location and are to be found in contact with one another but without necessary inter-relationships. Thanks to modern physics, the cosmos is seen as a vast enterprise in which there are innumerable foci of energy, whose existence is not in isolation from one another but rather in their capacity to 'contain' in a non-spatial fashion influences and affects from their environment.

Furthermore the world is such that each of its constituents is 'in process' – that is, each of them is essentially a direction taken towards making actual the potentialities which are integral to it. From a past which is inherited or received through significant choices (usually not conscious at 'lower' levels of energy) at the given moment, towards a future goal or end which in Process Thought is called 'subjective aim', each occasion plays its part in a more general 'creative advance'. Each focus is unique, because it has its particular inherited past, its particular given moment of choice, and its particular specific aim or end. Yet all of them are knitted together in a social world and none of them occurs in isolation from other occasions or events. Further, there is about such 'entities' (to use here Whitehead's own word) a certain novelty, more especially at the higher levels of the world process. At the lower levels, and in configurations which, like stones or similar objects, are more like accumulations than like genuinely societal associations, novelty is minimal; but as more complex and inclusive levels appear, novelty is more pronounced. Thus there is what A. S. Pringle-Pattison styled 'continuity of process, with the emergence of genuine novelty'.

Each of these foci has some measure of 'importance', which means that it has some value intrinsic or integral to its existence. That is, it plays its part in, and discloses in its own way, what is going on in the world. But certain events have a greater importance than others; these are more adequately revelatory of the general creative advance. In varying ways they gather up the past, are decisively active in the present, and aim towards future 'satisfaction' of potentiality, thus making it possible to see something of the general trend in the cosmos. They are bits of experience, using that word in its wider sense, with an objectivity and a subjectivity such as we know in our own introspection into how things are with us at the human level – and where else could we turn for such an insight, since human awareness, when deep and prolonged, is our one sure indication of how things do in fact go in the world?

I have already noted the interrelationship between events. The world is such that anything and everything affects or influences every other event. This takes place by what Whitehead called 'prehension' – a grasping or a feeling that receives into the particular event what is present in the past and then itself is grasped or felt by what follows. Hence in the prehensive movement time plays its part. We, and all else, have our existence in a world of succession, where all three tenses (past, present, and future) have significance and exercise a decisive power. Therefore, each event feels and employs past occasions for the realization of its own aim; and every succeeding event feels and uses that given occasion for *its* actualization.

In such a world, freedom is basic. At lower levels, in the realm of inanimate matter as well as in less complex instances of animate matter or life, the freedom is minimal. But as we move on in the cosmos, more and more this freedom becomes a matter of conscious decision, although it is never to be exercised in such a fashion that sheer anarchy is present. Freedom means a capacity to decide between possibilities. If a quantum of energy opts for *this* direction it has in fact 'decided' (a word whose Latin root, *decidere*, means 'to cut off') against *that* direction, although obviously not with awareness as we experience it. And decisions, with the varying degrees of freedom that are entailed, have consequences. To opt for one of several possibilities means that subsequent happenings are different from what they would have been if the option had been for another possibility. Yet such freedom does not contradict the wider ordering, as if each occurrence were entirely independent of all others. The societal nature of the world prevents this; and furthermore, there are 'rules' which govern the mode of the advance. Of course these rules are not externally laid down. They are integral to the whole movement in the cosmos; and they are more like the internal 'controls' that determine procedure in any given area of investigation, experiment, or observation, than they are like dictates from above or outside.

If what has just been said is the case, then all constituent events in the cosmos have a 'di-polar' nature. They include both abstract possibility and also the concrete actuality which has come into existence through decision on the basis of given data. And as we have noted above, all events have some importance or value, indicative of the basic thrust or drive which works creatively in the cosmos and provides the opportunity for novelty. But that importance is never imposed upon the event; it is integral to it, developing in greater degree as the capacity for prehension or grasping is greater.

Finally, persuasion is more effective in the long run than sheer coercion. Appearances may seem to tell us exactly the opposite. Yet the history of civilization, human thought, and experience at its highest, can be understood as a growing insight into this primacy of persuasion. The world religions, as Dr Trevor Ling has demonstrated in his valuable book *History of Religion East and West* (Macmillan), have moved from positions whose main stress has been on power or impersonal being or substance or cosmic order to one in which tenderness, benevolence, persuasion and love have been given central place. One instance of this, to which we shall give further attention in Chapter 6, is the tradition which we have inherited: that is, the Judaeo-Christian development as this is reported to us in the Old Testament, and in the event (with its consequences) of Jesus as this is witnessed to in the New Testament. But it is not only in the specifically religious sphere that insight into the primacy of persuasion or love has been found. The greatest poets, dramatists, sages, and seers, from all countries and from all cultures, have written, spoken, or sung in this fashion. Indeed we may agree here with Whitehead who once said that in his view the story of human history, more especially as it reached the status of advanced civilization, is the story of the various ways in which Plato's conviction, that persuasion rather than coercion is the clue to the way things go in the cosmos, has been anticipated or confirmed.

It should be understood, however, that the fact to which I have just called attention does not imply any necessary or inevitable progress, after the fashion of an automatic escalator on which one is carried from floor to floor up to the highest storey of a building. On the contrary, there are 'ups' and 'downs', retreats as well as advances. Today nobody can subscribe to the old-fashioned so-called liberal optimism of the late Victorian Age, although that period in history was nothing like so foolishly cheerful as later decades have assumed. Nor does evolution proceed directly and without deviation or distortion from evil towards good. But there *is* some genuine over-all advance, attained through anguish and characterized by tragedy; and realistic observation should not be supposed to tell us nothing but a story of degradation, increasing evil, and human wickedness.

The basic conviction of those who, like me, subscribe to the Process conceptuality is that the supreme reality which is the guarantor of order and the provider of novel possibilities, the source of the human sense of refreshment and cosmic companionship, the ground of our deep feeling that existence is significant and possesses genuine value, the chief but not the only causal agency, and the ultimate recipient of what has been accomplished in the world for good: that this reality, which religion calls God, is not the supreme anomaly without relationship to what we know about how things go. On the contrary this supreme reality is itself the 'chief exemplification', as Whitehead puts it, of the categories or explanatory principles which we have found necessary if we are to come to any proper interpretation of our own human experience and of the world in which that experience is had.

This brings us to our proposal, following Whitehead, of a new model of God which will be viable in the world which we know today to be our world. I shall present this model under seven headings.

1. To speak of God as the 'chief exemplification' rather than as the contradiction of the categories required to make sense of experience and the world, does not mean that God is characterized by such categories exactly as they stand in our finite experience. God is their *chief* exemplification; in him these categories have an eminent quality. Furthermore, God is everlasting, whereas all else is perishing. God does not perish; he exists through all time, through all temporal passage, through all historical change. Again, God alone includes within himself primordially all genuine possibility relevant to any occasion. He is supreme in goodness, in delight in that goodness, and in a receptivity which can harmonize the values achieved in the

creation. With *the creatures*, the initial state is what Process Thought styles 'physical', having to do with the matter-of-fact aspect, while the 'conceptual' or mental pole, with its capacity for decision and actualization is supervenient upon it; in God the conceptual is prior, since he knows all possibility and works for its actualization.

2. But if this be the case, what is the divine nature or character? Here we find in the new model a quite different approach from the traditional one. Whereas in the old model the emphasis has been on the divine *aseitas* or self-containedness and self-sufficiency of God apart from everything else, in the new model the stress is laid on relationship and entails the ontological reality of persuasion or love. The old model was dependent, as Whitehead himself urged, upon ideas of the 'ruling Caesar, the ruthless moralist, or the unmoved mover'; whatever was said about the divine character as loving was adjectival to these ideas. But the new model takes with utmost seriousness what Whitehead called 'the brief Galilean vision' which 'dwells upon the tender elements in the world, which slowly and in quietness operate by love'. Nor is this vision confined to the event of Christ, although that event is for us its definitive expression; and in our chapter on biblical thought we shall give considerable attention to this christological point. The vision is also found, in varying degrees of adequacy, in the human experience of loving relationships and in everything that upbuilds and enriches experience. In this vision, with its focus (so far as we can know) in the Christ-event, there is made possible the 'direct intuition' in a given 'special occasion', which provides for us a key or clue which is of wider generality and can be applied to 'the ordering of all occasion'. This point has been well made by Professor A. H. Johnson, one-time research student under Whitehead at Harvard, when he says that the picture of God, the model for deity, may therefore be seen as essentially a 'generalization' of what has been 'disclosed in act' in Jesus and in the response made to him, expressed in the subsequent witness to his impact upon men and women.

For Christian experience, the focus is upon a particular event which is taken to be of special importance because it emerges from a long history that prepared for its appearance, while at the same time it opens up for those who accept it a particular way of looking at the world and a particular way of grounding the human sense of worth. Thus the first assertion to be made about the new model is that it portrays God as essentially persuasive: 'God is Love'. This is not simply a human theory or a philosophical speculation; it has its basis in the event of Christ as responded to by others, and along with this in all similar human experience in which Love-in-Act is taken as important in a high degree.

3. This means that we reject notions of God as being entirely self-sufficient and self-contained. Love *is in* relationships. These relationships work both ways: from the lover to the one loved and from the one loved (who in responding begins to realize the capacity to love) to the initiating lover. Thus God is intimately related to and affected by the world. He is both creative and responsive, as Cobb and Griffin have urged in their book already mentioned. To say this is not to deny divine transcendence, once this is understood as meaning not remoteness nor unaffectedness but rather inexhaustibility, enduring faithfulness, and the capacity to absorb the sting of evil and turn what seemed (and indeed was) wrong into an occasion for further and perhaps even greater good. At the same time, however, divine immanence is asserted, precisely because Love, divine Love, is at work *in the world*, providing lures towards increasing good and overcoming that which is distorted and wrong by its indefatigable concern for the excellent as it can be achieved in any given instance.

We shall give more attention to these and other important matters in succeeding chapters. Here it will suffice to say that the model we have proposed is neither a deistic view of God as entirely disassociated from and entirely independent of the world, nor is it a pantheistic view in which God and the world are identified. We are not talking about *deus sive natura*, in Spinoza's phrase; God and world are not the same reality seen from different perspectives. In the new model we have an identification by God *with* his world, not an identity of God *and* the world. The created order exists by what Whitehead called 'its incarnation' of God in various ways, at different times, and with expressions that are appropriate for the several levels and differing circumstances of that world.

4. Traditional theology has found it difficult to admit that God can be acted upon or affected by what goes on in the creation. For that theology, the creation is indeed in a real relationship with God since he was its creator and it depends upon him for its continuing existence. But as I pointed out in our earlier discussion, for that theology God has only a logical relationship with the world as its one and only causal agent. It can give nothing to God and in no sense is he seriously affected by it. We may find it difficult to see how God, so conceived, could be called 'loving'. This is the basic paradox in the traditional theology which it has never been able to resolve and about which it can only speak as a 'mystery' – which in this case is much more an absurd contradiction than a recognition of the infinite depths of the divine Love.

For the new model, since all existence (in any instance of our experience or observation) is a 'becoming' and a 'belonging' – a process which is societal in character – God himself as the chief exemplification of such categories is taken to be the supreme instance of becoming *and* of belonging. The former is a way of insisting that he is not to be envisaged as so much above temporal succession that history is irrelevant to him; on the contrary, God is participant in succession, yet remains constant and faithful in his own character as Love.

The latter (belonging) is true of God precisely because he is so related to the world that there is between him and that world a 'give-and-take'. He is the giver of aims and the lure towards their actualization; so, also, he is the recipient of what happens when those aims are on the way to realization. At every point, the occasions in the world make their contribution to the divine life, whether for a fuller divine satisfaction or for an anguished divine reception. He is influenced by what happens. 'Things matter to him and they have their consequences in him', as Whitehead himself once put it.

5. But this does not mean that God is (so to say) 'getting to be more divine'. He is always and everywhere unsurpassable by anything which is not himself; yet he can surpass himself as he was in earlier states of relationship with the world by what he comes to experience in later states. So God remains God, but he is always God *with his world*, rejoicing in its achievements and suffering from its failures. There are distortions, deviations, back-waters, and rejections in that world. The fact of evil, thus interpreted, is a real fact with which we must reckon. Therefore the divine experience, like that of the created occasions, is a tragic one. But evil is not willed by God; he wills only that which is good. Nor is it 'permitted' by him, as if things could be otherwise. It is erroneous to think of God as responsible for what goes wrong in creation, save in the sense that he respects all created freedom and works with all created causes. To be free in any genuine sense entails the possibility, as a *given* in the creative advance, that there shall be drags, back-waters, self-centred contentment, and the like, which constitute the evil that we know from our own experience to be altogether appalling and terrible. God combats this evil; he shares in the anguish which it brings about; and in his 'consequent' aspect, as a concrete actuality in continuing relationship with the world, he can and does strive ceaselessly and effectually to transmute such evil into an opportunity for good.

6. I have just mentioned God's consequent aspect. This brings us to the distinctions which Whitehead and others have made, with God envisaged as primordial, as consequent, and as superjective. To call

these 'natures', as Whitehead did on occasion, was a careless lapse in language, since what he intended to indicate were differing ways in which God may be envisaged by us and not to speak of diverse divine 'existences'.

To say that God is primordial is to say that he contains within himself the whole continuum of possibility. In this aspect, he is purely conceptual, but is yet the basis of all actuality. He is not *before* creation but *with* creation, as Whitehead put it. But the existence of a creation, given in our experience, requires a creative principle. To speak of a creator without a creation, or of a creation without a creator, is to engage in linguistic nonsense.

When God is said to be consequent, reference is being made to him as related to, and affected by, the created order. This is God in his concrete actuality as encountered in various ways, usually under what may appropriately be styled an incognito since he does not announce himself in any obvious fashion but works normally through his secular functioning in the world. God has provided the creation with its aims, out of his primordial aspect; but he lures it towards the achievement of these aims and receives responsively into his own life what is done there. So in his concrete actuality he has been, is, and will be influenced by that doing. In the result, nothing will be lost that can be 'saved'; and this is because God can harmonize apparent contradictions, prevent significant contrasts from becoming destructive conflicts, and in his wisdom use that which in fact has taken place for further advancement of his intention of Love. For a Christian, the paradigm here would be Good Friday suffused with the light of Easter morning.

Finally, as superjective, God contributes to the ongoing of the cosmic advance what he himself is and what he has received from the world once this has been transmuted in his own life. As a friend of mine has put it, 'In his superjective aspect, God offers back to the world, for its own employment, everything of value from the past, so that it may be used for the formation of the future.' Thus there is throughout the process the give-and-take to which I referred earlier. Yet always the initiative is from God, who provides the possibilities, seeks for opportunities for novelty, lures the created occasions to actualize them, and as those respond to his invitation or solicitation, enjoys what they are enabled to bring about.

7. Much of what has been said in this chapter may seem very abstract. But I am convinced that when we look deeply into ourselves we shall find that in our experience there are intimations of just the sort of world that I have described. At no point is this more obvious than in the basic religious emphasis in the new model of God. That

emphasis, of course, is on God as primarily and essentially Love-in-Act in relation to his creation.

We must consider later the ways in which the traditional talk about the divine attributes, metaphysical, relational and moral, may suitably be interpreted when the new model is adopted. Here I say only briefly that to talk, for instance, of omnipotence is to speak of the divine Love as the only enduringly strong and never-failing reality. To speak of omnipresence is to say that the divine Love is available at all times and to all creatures, under whatever 'disguises' it may be manifested. To say that God is omniscient is to affirm that the divine Love is possessed of the wisdom and understanding which love alone can have.

I conclude, however, by saying more about love itself. It is this which makes the new model attractive; it is this which gives that model its religious significance. We must be sure that the word 'love' is not taken in its weak sense. Rather, it must be understood as a strong word. Love is demanding and it can be terrifying to those of us – indeed, to all of us – who are fearful of the kind of caring which will never rest content with cheap, shoddy, sentimental, or merely emotional response. Love, as the central reality of God, is gracious yet demanding, generous yet inexorable, as ready to receive as it is to give, always participating in the other's experience.

We shall see later that the Bible portrays God as living, loving, active, concerned and recipient. The Jewish people learned this through their long and troubled history. They began by seeing God as power. They moved on, under Moses, to see him as righteous. Through the prophets (and more particularly through such men as Hosea and Jeremiah), they came to understand him as loving-kindness. Then came Jesus, in whom (as Christian belief would declare) divine Loving was definitely enacted and expressed through a human loving that sought human response. In other religious traditions there has been something of the same movement, from 'God the void, through God the enemy, to God the companion', in Whitehead's telling words. In divers fashions, the deepest human insight has been that the reality behind phenomena is more than beneficent: rather, it has been that this reality is sheer Love-in-action.

The chief benefit from the new model of God, so far as working religion in its worship and belief and discipleship is concerned, is in its putting 'pure unbounded Love' at the heart of things. Perhaps we can say succinctly that this new model is essentially an affirmation that Love is *absolutely central in the universe*. Along with material drawn from philosophical thinking, scientific discovery, aesthetic and moral awareness, and whatever else is deepest in human experience, this insight makes sense for us, even as it challenges us to respond by lives in which creaturely loving is wrought out in word and deed and thought. Thornton Wilder, in *The Bridge of San Luis Rey* (Longman), spoke for all that is best in our human understanding when he said that 'Love is the only survival, the only meaning.'

Notes on Whitehead and Hartshorne

Since this book is a presentation and commendation of what in the title of the present chapter I have called Whitehead's proposal of a new model for God, it may be helpful to the reader if something is said about the man whose proposal is being discussed. Many in his own country, England, are not very familiar with Whitehead's life, work, and influence; happily, in North America this is not the case, for on that continent Whitehead is a name to be reckoned with, both in philosophical and theological circles.

Alfred North Whitehead was born on 15 February 1861 at Ramsgate in Kent, where his father was vicar of a parish after some years spent as a schoolmaster. He died in Cambridge, Massachusetts, in the United States, on 30 December 1947, at the ripe age of eighty-six.

In childhood he was taught by his father; then he attended Sherborne, the ancient boys' school in Dorset which he liked to remember as having been founded by St Aldhelm in 741. He went up to Trinity College, Cambridge, in 1880; in 1885 he was admitted a Fellow of that college. His speciality was mathematics, although he had studied Greek, Latin, history, and literature at Sherborne; and he never lost interest in what broadly may be styled 'the humanities'. He remained at Cambridge, eventually as lecturer in mathematics, until 1910. After a year spent in writing, he began teaching at University College, London, and in 1914 became a professor at the Imperial College of Science and Technology of the University of London. He served in administrative posts in the university and towards the end of his London period was president of its Senate. In 1924, he accepted an appointment as Professor of Philosophy at Harvard University in the United States. He retired from that post in the mid-thirties, but continued to live in Cambridge, America, where Harvard is located.

Whitehead's first publications were in mathematics. Later he delivered lectures at Cambridge, England and elsewhere in Britain on the philosophy of science; his Tanner lectures at Cambridge appeared under the title of *The Concept of Nature* (Cambridge University Press) in 1919. He was associated with his former pupil at Trinity College, Bertrand Russell, in the preparation of the three volumes of the famous *Principia Mathematica* (1910–1913) (Cambridge University Press 1962). It was not until his Harvard days that he turned to philosophical lecturing and writing on a wider scale; some of the books that he wrote and published while there are listed below. The most lengthy – and most difficult – of these is *Process and Reality*, the Gifford Lectures at Edinburgh, which he delivered in 1927–28.

It must be recognized, of course, that his thought had antecedents. These included the recent developments in physics, some acquaintance with other evolutionary thinkers (Alexander and Lloyd Morgan in Britain and Bergson in France), and of course his own moral, aesthetic, and religious experience. None the less, it was strikingly original.

A fuller sketch of his life appears in my *Alfred North Whitehead: A Maker of Contemporary Theology* (Lutterworth, London and John Knox, Virginia 1969), which also includes a more adequate outline of his philosophical position. Perhaps the best popular presentation of his views may be found in two volumes entitled *Whitehead's Theory of Reality* and *Whitehead's Philosophy of Civilization*, by Professor A. H. Johnson, a former research student under him at Harvard. Both of these are Dover Paperbacks, originally published in 1952 and 1958 respectively but reprinted many times thereafter.

I trust that an idea of his general conceptuality is given in the course of the chapters of the present book. The way in which this viewpoint has been used in theological circles, especially in the United States, may be learned from my *Lure of Divine Love* (T. & T. Clark, Edinburgh and Pilgrim Press, New York 1979) and Peter N. Hamilton's *The Living God and the Modern World* (Hodder and Stoughton, London and Pilgrim Press, New York 1967), both written in Britain; and from a great number of American volumes, notably *The Reality of God*, by Schubert Ogden (SCM Press, London and Harper & Row New York 1967) and most recently *Process Theology: An Introductory Exposition*, by John Cobb and David Griffin (Christian Journals Press, Belfast and Westminster Press, Philadelphia 1976).

The books from Whitehead that appeared during his Harvard period and have been most influential in Christian theological circles in North America are:

Science and the Modern World (The Free Press 1925)
Religion in the Making (New American Library 1926)
Process and Reality (The Free Press 1929)
The Adventures of Ideas (Macmillan 1933 and The Free Press
   1967)
Modes of Thought (The Free Press 1938)

In my presentation of the new model for God, I have followed the
thought of Whitehead. But I should like here to add a short treatment
of the development of Whiteheadian thought which may be found in
the writings of the American philosopher Charles Hartshorne. Hartshorne has made a significant contribution to the development of the
new model, not least in what he himself has styled the 'di-polar' view
of deity.

In working out this view, Hartshorne calls attention to a third
alternative which differs from the either/or of traditional thinking.
For such traditional thinking, God was either completely absolute in
all respects, or there was nothing conceivable which was not entirely
relative and hence contingent. But Hartshorne insists that there is a
third possibility: a given entity may be absolute in some respects and
relative in others. Such a possibility seems not to have dawned upon
earlier thinkers in any very clear way, although Hartshorne thinks
that there have been intimations of this view from time to time in the
history of thought.

How does this work out? It is just here that Hartshorne makes his
interesting development of Whiteheadian thinking about a model for
God. He proposes that we recognize that there is an element of
profound truth in the notion of 'absolute' but that it has usually been
misapplied. Instead of looking at God as absolute because in him
there is nothing save the eternal, unchanging, sheerly transcendent,
and the like, it is possible to see that the absolute quality of God
consists in his being always and unchangingly loving, faithful, good,
and righteous. God may also be seen as unchanging in the sense that
he is always and everywhere in relationship with the creation, so that
at no point and at no time could he be conceived as other than so
related.

On the other hand, once that kind of absoluteness is granted, God
is also relative, or relational, both in himself and in his ways of acting.
He is affected and influenced by what occurs in the world. He does
not exist in separation from that world – although he is distinct from
it by virtue of his being an actual entity and because of the unsurpas-
sibility which is proper to him in respect to his never perishing, to his
everlastingness, and to his capacity to receive into his own life that

which is contributed by the world and its activity. It is important here for us to see the difference between distinction and separation, a difference often overlooked by theologians and philosophers. On the one hand, there is no God without *a* world; but it need not be *this* world, since others are conceivable where diverse 'styles of creation' might obtain. On the other hand, to speak in that vein need not entail the idea that God and the world are identical; nor need it assume that there is not an asymmetry between the two. God is the ever-faithful, ever-loving, ever-related reality; the world is finite, always changeable and perishing.

Much of what I have summarized in this note will have been found in the main body of this chapter, although phrased in a different manner. The merit of Hartshorne's position is that it enables us to recognize that there was a partial insight in earlier models of God but that this insight was not grasped in its proper meaning. Thus in our proposal for a new model of God, derived chiefly from the 'Galilean vision' but with sources also in philosophical, scientific and existential understanding, we may profit from what earlier thinkers have said and written – provided we make the requisite correction in their way of applying such terms as absolute, eternal, and the like.

Finally, Hartshorne is a vigorous defender of a philosophical approach to theological matters. His metaphysics could best be described as a metaphysics of love; and in this respect he would be entirely in agreement with the line taken in this chapter and indeed in this book as a whole.

A Note on God as Love

'God is Love', so the Johannine text says. But as we have already suggested and as we shall insist in the sequel, such an affirmation cannot be made if we assume (as many might well do) that the 'Love' about which we are here talking is identical with, in every respect the same as, the love which we know in our human experience and relationships. That love, humanly experienced and known, must be our starting-place. But when we speak of *God* as Love, we must recognize that there is inevitably a difference. Or, to use a word made familiar in recent years through the writings of the late Ian Ramsey, love must in this instance have a 'qualifier'.

Ramsey's point, made over and over again in his writings, is really quite simple. When we are speaking, so far as we are able to speak, of matters pertaining to deity, we need to understand that there is a quality or characteristic of the divine which is above and beyond anything that is strictly human. Thus, to call God creator is to speak of him in terms drawn from human understanding, but it is also necessary to speak of him in an 'eminent sense', to use the idiom of the middle ages. God *is* creator; but he is creator in a much more exalted way than any creative activity in our experience might suggest. Thus it is necessary to qualify what we say by recognizing always that the reference is to God and not to our human level of experience.

In the present context, then, I wish to insist that when we use as our model for God the idea of the Lover, the cosmic Lover, the very word 'cosmic' carries with it the understanding that here we have to do with a notion of love which is beyond the limitations, defects, imperfections, and lacks that of necessity characterize our human awareness of love. The biblical way of saying this is to talk about God as 'holy Love'. Without such qualification, we might seem to be identifying God as Lover with the love which we know in human relationships; we might seem to suggest that God is to be modelled after that human love but without any distinctions or differences. To do that would be to confuse creator and creation, the sinless and the imperfect, the complete and the partial. That mistake would result in the loss of the transcendence of God – his being inexhaustible, indefatigable, indefeasible, and perfect as Lover.

I trust that in what has so far been said, as well as in what is to be said hereafter in this book, it will be clear that no such reduction of the divine to the human is intended. When we say God, we mean that which, or him who, is entirely worshipful, unsurpassable by anything not himself, dependable, adorable, and supreme. This should already have been apparent. But it is necessary to insist upon the point here, lest there be misunderstanding and misinterpretation of what is entailed in our proposal. And one way in which the correct view can be presented is through the use of such qualifiers as Ramsey believed to be required in any and every model when it is used in our talking about God.

In the medieval period and in other periods, and with other types of Christian theology than the one that is being urged in this book, the same end was sought by the recognition that we can only speak of the divine reality analogically. Or in the language preferred by modern theologians like Paul Tillich, the reference to God must be of a symbolic nature. But whatever the idiom, the point ought to be plain enough. There is no exact identification, no precise identity, between ideas, notions, concepts, or models which derive from the human realm (as they must, if we are to talk at all) and the divine reality to which they point and which they seek to indicate.

Perhaps this warning is not necessary in the context within which we are speaking, but it seems none the less important to make it quite evident. A friend of mine once spoke scathingly of the way in which some modern writers have appeared to say that God and man are identical or (as I once put it) that 'man at his best equalled God'. I should then add that it must be 'God at his worst'! Any such view is both blasphemous and absurd. God is always God, nothing more and nothing less. Things of the created order are exactly that – they are *created*, with the limitations proper to them. We can speak of God in idiom drawn from the human realm, but we must always do this with a difference.

5

Experiential, Philosophical, and Scientific Background

In the development of the new model of God presented in the preceding chapter, the basic ingredient – at least so far as Christian theological interest is concerned – has been what Whitehead called 'the brief Galilean vision', in the phrase we have already quoted. This is appropriate, since after all talk about God is inevitably religious talk, having to do with the unsurpassable and dependable reality whom we address in prayer, adore in liturgical worship, and find to be a source of strength and 'an ever present help in time of trouble', as well as the grounding for our sense that human existence has worth and significance.

The chapters which follow this one will be devoted to a consideration of that specifically religious ingredient. But for the moment it will be well to concern ourselves with certain other important considerations. We may ask, therefore, what kind of wider experiential basis there may be for modelling God in the fashion we have suggested. We may enquire what philosophical considerations are significant in this connection. And we may ask to what degree contemporary scientific enquiry and its assured results are in accordance with such a model or, at the very least, do not conflict with what is proposed – unlike the position in respect to the old model, with which they seem often to be in plain contradiction.

Perhaps the best way to get at the first of these questions is through some discussion of what it feels like to be a humanly existing creature. In other words, when we look into ourselves and attempt to understand what it is that makes us think, feel, and act humanly, what do we discover? What emerges may then be generalized and used as a clue to other areas or dimensions of the world-order. That procedure, in fact, is the one followed by Process thinkers, when with Whitehead, the 'founding father' of that kind of philosophy, they insist that the one point about which we have intimate knowledge is found precisely in our experience of what it is like to be human.

Surely one of the first things that we know about ourselves is that we are not finished articles, entirely complete and settled. On the contrary, we are dynamic agents and as such we are instances of 'becoming'. Each of us feels himself or herself to be moving towards, or away from, a fulfilment of some possibility. We are 'on the way'; we have not arrived. Robert Browning wrote 'Man never is/But wholly hopes to be. . .'. And something of that insight is verified for us as we look into ourselves.

When we do thus look into ourselves, we also recognize that we are inheritors of a past which has gone into making us what we are at the moment. None of us can escape this heredity. Nor is it confined simply to our physical constitution; it includes our racial memory, all that we have been led to think or believe, the patterns of behaviour which have been taught us, and a great deal else which is inescapable and causally effectual upon us. We have come into existence at a given time and place, to be sure; but that very fact involves us in a situation where we are dependent upon what has gone before us and which, as I have urged, has done almost everything to make us what we happen to be.

At the same time, however, we see ourselves as responsible agents who are called upon to make choices which are relevant to what we have received and to what future may be open for us. This means that we have some awareness, however vague or dim this may be, that there are goals or aims which lure us towards their achievement. The direction of our existence is essentially towards realizing fully such possibilities as may be ours; and while in a narrower sense this may be towards a particular vocation, job, or situation, in a broader sense we can say that we are conscious of the impulsion to become more fully and genuinely human – we are called to become what we have it in us to be. But we do not and cannot move forward save in association with our fellow men and women. For we are social creatures, who belong with others, who depend largely upon what those others can provide for us, and who in our turn are contributory to them in their movement forward.

Thus we are historical creatures. The past which is ours is inescapably there, to be sure, and it provides us with the materials upon which we are able to make decisions towards a future. But it is in the present moment, whether narrowly or more broadly conceived, that decisions are made. To be able to decide, however, requires that we have genuine freedom. Unless our decisions are entirely automatic or imposed, they are always between or among possible alternatives. Obviously the extent of those alternatives is not unlimited. Where we are and what we are, the times and places and circumstances of our present existence, and a great deal else which unavoidably locates us in a here-and-now, will impose real limits upon our freedom. None the less, that freedom exists; and denial of it produces absurdity. For everybody acts as if he or she did indeed possess some degree of freedom in terms of which decision is made; in the words of C. D. Broad, the Cambridge philosopher of the last generation, denial of such freedom and of the ability to decide in its light is one of those 'silly notions which only a very clever person could have thought up'. Or we may agree with Bishop Joseph Butler who in *The Analogy of Religion* (R. West) argues for the freedom of the will by noting that since everybody acts as if it were so, and assumes that others act in the same fashion, it would be an absurd contradiction to deny that this freedom exists and that we do in fact possess it.

If our past is significant and if our present moment of choice is equally significant, so also is the future towards which we are moving. Humans live *towards* the future, just as much as they live *from* the past and *in* the present. The future may be feared or it may be awaited with eagerness; but we always have hopes about it and we exist with reference to it.

We humans also have a feeling of accountability about what we have chosen and where we are going as a consequence of our choices. There are moments when any of us may very well feel that he is helpless and hence not responsible for what 'the changes and chances of this mortal life' bring about. Certainly that is a common enough experience. Yet much more profound in human experience is the sense that things could have gone otherwise and that we ourselves have had a significant part in making them go in the way they have gone. Our life together in human society is predicated upon this sense of accountability; and while there may be, and often are, extenuating factors, we are unwilling entirely to abrogate that feeling and place all the blame, or all the credit, upon other persons or upon circumstances. 'I might have done this or that', we say; and we either regret what we believe to have been our own decision or we rejoice in it as having been, at the moment, the proper one to have made.

So far, emphasis has been placed on our knowledge and our will or conational power. But there is also our emotional life, in the deep sense of 'feeling-tone' and aesthetic awareness. We know ourselves to be creatures who appreciate negatively or positively this or that occasion which we experience or with which we are confronted. We make valuations, saying that this or that possibility is good or bad, better or worse. We respond to things that we consider beautiful – which is to say, harmonious and lovely or lovable. In much talk about human nature this side of experience has been given less than its due place. Education has been intellectual and discipline has been concerned with volition; not so much has been said about the way in which art, for example, can contribute enormously to the proper development of human existence, the enrichment of life, and the deepening of experience.

We are *becoming* and we are *belonging*. We are also *thinking* and *feeling* creatures. We are embodied beings, too, in that our physical nature very importantly plays its part towards realizing our proper humanity. Much religious teaching, alas, has been altogether too spiritual or mental, and too little physical or sensual. Yet we are all aware of the way in which bodily states influence mental and spiritual states; the reverse is also true. Our thinking and our spiritual capacity can affect and be affected by our bodies – all this is clear enough in what is known today about psychosomatics. Even in such supposedly spiritual attitudes as love, friendship, caring, and even casual acquaintanceships, our bodies are involved. In other books I have suggested that all such relationships with others, even with God when we are concerned with the divine dimension in the world, have their physiological-psychological base in the pervasive sexuality which is tied in with our bodily existence. The desire to be intimately at one with another, even when it is not accompanied by specific genital contact or the wish to engage in such contact, includes deep human feeling-tones which have their grounding in our physical nature with its sexual equipment and all that goes with it.

Finally, there is in human experience a feeling that we are in some sense being made for a destiny that is not exhausted by the immediacies of our day-to-day living. The biblical text which says that 'God has set eternity in our hearts' points to a profound truth, even for the non-religiously minded person. That person, like all the rest of us, is aware that there is a 'more' which beckons us, however we may wish to define that 'more'. Human existence is never complete, never entirely fulfilled. 'Our hearts are in disquietude', as St Augustine said, because we know that we cannot rest content in the ordinary mundane realities which surround us and engage most, but never all, of ourselves.

With this there goes a persisting sense of human imperfection, even of human distortion of right and proper growth. We are finite and we are going to die; this we know and in our acceptance of it we are aware both of the fact that our life is mortal and that we must see ourselves as creatures that are certain to perish. But above and beyond this, there is what Thoreau called the 'sense of desperation' which now and again overwhelms us, maybe during sleepless nights when we are brought face to face with our truest selves and our inadequacies, imperfections, and failures. Such moments of experience tell us that we are placed in a world which cannot entirely satisfy our profound desires and that even in our efforts to find such satisfaction we are all too prone to seek for it in ways that ultimately will not provide the very thing we want: true, genuine, proper actualization of our real selfhood.

Existential analysis of human existence, as this is known to each of us, produces some such picture as I have just sketched. It may very well provide us with a clue to how things go in the world at large. In the last chapter I gave a summary outline of the sort of world that nowadays most informed people understand this one to be. I shall not repeat that outline here. But it seems apparent from human experience itself, once we have taken it with great seriousness, that we are led to recognize that the wider world is dynamic, processive, temporal, societal, moving towards goals which may be denied or rejected – a world incapable of fulfilling itself but requiring some 'more' in which satisfaction may ultimately be found. There is every reason to think that the insight which an analysis of our own sense of being human makes possible for us is an indication of something much more general. It is odd that so many thinkers have sought to understand that wider world by a study of physical nature, by logical argument, or in some other intellectual fashion, but have entirely neglected the human experience which for all of us is the one thing that we know most intimately and about which we can speak with most adequacy. Now that we know that human life is 'organic to the cosmos', as evolutionary science has taught us, and that our human life is in fact an emergent from the natural order and cannot properly be interpreted apart from it, we have the more reason to say the converse too: that the world at large, the natural order, the wider reaches of the cosmos, cannot rightly be interpreted if we fail to take with utmost seriousness what we know about *ourselves* and about how *we* go in that setting. In a day when human existence was taken to be a drama acted out on a stage, and everything else was simply stage-setting without direct relevance to that drama, it might have made sense to engage in what Whitehead called 'false bifurcation' between human existence and cosmic generality. But ours is not that day; and we should have learned the lesson.

So much, then, for some consideration of the experiential aspect as this is disclosed in our human existence. We now turn to philosophical matters and see how things stand in that area.

In an earlier chapter a good deal has been said about such philosophical matters. I need make here only a few points which are relevant to the approach to the new model of God. One of these has to do with what I shall call 'metaphysics in a new mode'.

In older philosophy, the arguments for God were worked out with care and with as much logical rigour as was possible. The cosmological argument proceeded by attempting to show that a world which is contingent, finite, dependent, and created, could not have come into existence unless there were a necessary, infinite, and uncreated being who willed that it should exist. The teleological argument began from the reality of purpose in the creation. In its less sophisticated form, as with Archdeacon William Paley, it argued from such instances as a watch which requires a watchmaker; and in its more sophisticated form, it found wider traces of purpose throughout the world which pointed towards a divine, that is to say a non-finite and non-temporal, purposive being. The ontological argument, in many ways the most difficult to understand, insisted that the very idea of an infinite perfect being itself entailed the existence of such a being. Descartes phrased it in that fashion. Anselm, the medieval ecclesiastic and theologian, put it in a somewhat different way. For him the fact that we can conceive of a being beyond whom nothing greater can be thought carried with it the corollary that such a being must exist or else our conception would be 'greater' than what was in truth the case; and that was absurd. I believe that Barth was correct in saying that the Anselmian argument was more an articulation of the meaning found in worship than a satisfactory logical argument. Professor Charles Hartshorne, however, finds that in a somewhat modified form, following what he has called Anselm's 'revised argument', it still carries conviction – once we have defined deity as meaning not absolute in all respects, but absolute-relative, along the lines suggested in our last chapter.

However that may be, and with the recognition that for some other thinkers like the great scholastic theologian St Thomas Aquinas there were refinements in argument so that not three but five 'demonstrations' were proposed (excluding the ontological argument which Thomas rejected), the most that such argumentation can do is not to prove conclusively but to point towards the high probability of a divine reality. Even so, the argument for deity in such philosophical discussion usually gives us a concept of a divine being which is essentially that of the older model. On the other hand, it is doubtless

possible to say that if one already has some viable religious concept
of deity, the arguments may point to certain truths that can be
affirmed about that deity: God is necessary if there is to be a world at
all; God is the purposer who is working out that purpose in the
world; God is in some profound sense perfect (although as we have
seen there is ambiguity in what is to be understood by 'perfect'); and
God is the greatest conceivable one, beyond whom thought cannot
go. All of this presupposes that we have some notion of 'God' to
begin with. Aquinas illustrates this, since at the conclusion of each of
his 'ways' he says something of this sort: 'And all men call this God'.
But do they? Or can they, unless they already have some meaningful
and experiential notion of what the word 'God' signifies?

This then is metaphysics in the older and more conventional mode.
The new mode, however, which in my opinion is much more
convincing, does not proceed in that somewhat gradiose fashion with
its extraordinary confidence in human reason and its ability to prove
such deity. On the contrary it begins with the observable facts of
experience, with experiment, and with study of the world of nature
and history. In the light of what in such experience and study is
disclosed to us, it then attempts to work out some more comprehensive scheme which does not pretend to be omnicompetent but which
is more like an intimation and hint. In fact, it is not a system or scheme
at all; it is a *vision* of the world and how things go in that world.
Beginning from concrete experience and observation, it seeks for the
categories which will help towards an understanding of the 'going' of
that world. It is subject to correction; it is always to be referred back
to the experience and observation from which it starts so that it may
be confirmed or refuted. Whitehead has a homely illustration of this
procedure. He says that it is like an aviator who is familiar with the
place from which he is to begin his flight. The aviator takes off and
observes what is below him on his journey. He then returns to his
starting-place and seeks to find whether the intervening observation
bears any resemblance to what he knows concretely from his own
point of departure and arrival. In other words, he asks if it all 'fits
together', makes sense, and is coherent and consistent with what is
known to be actual fact.

This type of metaphysical inquiry is never final and complete; at
best it is suggestive and provides us with intimations that are to be
taken seriously and applied to as many areas or fields of knowledge
as are open to our investigation. In that fashion, the model of God is
not simply a logical construction but is the reality felt to be necessary
to explain what we already know. It is not the contradiction or denial
of the various principles drawn from experience and observation; it

is their 'chief exemplification', in the words from Whitehead which I have cited on earlier pages. It makes sense of those principles and they make sense of it, despite the eminent or superior manner in which they are exemplified in deity.

Unlike the older type of metaphysical understanding of God, the type which is here advocated is able to point to 'referends' which verify what is being said about God. The start is made from common human experience as it is known and lived in the sort of world which is familiar to us. What is more, it includes in its procedure the recognition in our experience of the appreciative, valuational, and emotional; that is, the 'feeling-tones' which are so much part of our human existence. Taking this deeply-experienced awareness of what it means to be human as the starting-point, we have every right to generalize from what that experience tells us and see whether it can be given wider application. If it can do this – always, of course, with what I should style 'rough edges' and not with complete, precise, and exact correspondence – then it has every claim to be accepted and the generalizations drawn from it affirmed with considerable confidence.

I have spoken of human observation. This brings us to the final topic of the present chapter: the scientific world-view which is now generally accepted by informed persons. It is to be granted, of course, that there is no entirely agreed world-view among scientific research-ers and investigators; but there is *enough* agreement to make it possible for us to speak meaningfully of what science, in its many various fields, has to tell us about the cosmos. In *that* sense, what has contemporary science to say?

First of all, we no longer hear about a world which resembles some vast machine. The earlier scientific view was that the cosmos was made up of bits of matter in motion, bumping up against each other, or forming configurations or masses which were in space-and-time and could be 'located' at given moments and in given places. The newer physics has altered all this. Nowadays, thanks to the quantum theory, the principle of indeterminacy, and relativity physics, we hear about 'fields' and not about simple location. We have learned that the cosmos is not composed of bits of matter in motion; it is made up, if that is the right way of putting it, of energies or charges whose behaviour is not precisely predictable, although, within certain limits, regularities may be observed in their behaviour. Furthermore, each such instance includes its environment in that it does not 'exist' in an absolutely self-contained fashion. I remember a physicist who illus-trated this to me by dropping a pencil on his desk, saying that because of that apparently insignificant act, the entire universe, to its remotest reaches, had been affected and changed – although he added, with a smile, that the amount of affect and change in that particular instance was infinitesimal. But even if infinitesimal, it was very real.

Again, instead of the universe seen as devoid of novelty, so that at least theoretically it would be possible to predict what was to happen as well as to describe what had happened, modern evolutionary science has plenty of room for novelty. It is an epigenetic process, not a mechanical one. It is not a matter of reshuffling previously existing bits of matter, but a process in which through rearrangement of pattern and introduction of new possibility there are 'emergents', which are not simply the earlier stuff with a slight difference in ordering, but a genuinely new reality. The world is indeed marked by continuity and consistency; but this has now been expanded to include within it what newly emerges with its own characteristics and qualities. Thus, in the simplest possible example, hydrogen and oxygen in appropriate combination produce water, which has its own distinctive nature such as neither hydrogen nor oxygen in themselves possess.

This 'continuity-with-novelty' can be applied, not only to the physical and chemical world, but also to the biological realm. There are newer scientific disciplines which have been able to work in this fashion across the older divisions; we have biophysics, biochemistry, molecular biology, and the like. Here there is no doubt about the continuities; but as such world-famous investigators as Dr W. H. Thorpe of Cambridge, the late Dr Theodosius Dubzhansky and Professor Ian Barbour in the United States, Dr Charles Birch of Sydney in Australia, and many others have demonstrated, there is also a novelty about living matter, and above all about living matter at its conscious human level, a novelty which must be taken into account in any accurate reporting about phenomena.

There is no space here to discuss the widely publicized and hence familiar contributions of study in the psychological realm, save to say that from the dynamic psychologists we have had assurances regarding the developmental quality of human experience and resultant behaviour, while the so-called 'depth psychologists' and psychoanalysts have helped us to understand the motivations, the complex patterns of human emotional life, and the ways in which men and women grow to maturity by accepting their past experiences and building them into new attitudes and modes of behaviour.

In summary, then, we can conclude that contemporary science gives us an 'open universe' in which 'possibility' is present and in which risks may be taken, growth may occur, and new things may happen. There is nothing in that newer science which rules out a conception of God which sees him as the chief exemplification of necessary categories of explanation; as chief causal agency working through created causes so that 'things can make themselves', in the phrase of the French philosopher Leguier; and as the final recipient of what is accomplished in the cosmos – indeed as the basic thrust and drive through that cosmos, whose innermost nature may very well be disclosed to us in important moments in the experience of the human race and in its history.

Modern science is increasingly coming to take an organic view of the world, in contrast to the mechanistic view so frequently adopted fifty and more years ago. This led in Whitehead's own time to Bergson's 'creative evolution' and Lloyd Morgan's 'emergent evolution', to take but two developments.

Analysis of the deliverances of human experience, philosophical considerations, and the newer understanding of the scientific enterprise combine to give us a secular background for the model of God with which we are concerned in this book. But obviously they do not compel belief in that model nor faith in God as God is portrayed there. As I have already said, no amount of argument can coerce faith, neither can such argument prove (in the sense of infallibly demonstrate) God's existence. In the last chapter of this book I shall have more to say about this, especially with regard to the 'adventure of faith', which is not contrary to human reason but goes beyond anything that such reason is able to provide. For our present purpose, it has been sufficient at this point simply to show that there are enough experiential, philosophical, and scientific data to make that adventure possible and to give it some significant grounding in the world which we know and which to some degree we can understand.

Whitehead himself spoke of physics as having to do with organisms of a less complicated sort and biology with those of a more complicated sort. Psychology helps us along the same lines; and the psychosomatic picture confirms this. But all organic existence is more a matter of persuasion and influence, mutually experienced, than of sheer coercive power. Once again, we are moving towards the emphasis on persuasion and love, or, in Teillard's splendid word, towards 'amorization', as the key or clue to reality.

6

The Biblical Data

In presenting the new model for deity, I pointed out that one way of stating it was to say that we have here a generalization of that which was disclosed in act in the event of Jesus Christ. So Professor A. H. Johnson has described the Whiteheadian vision of God. I believe that he is correct insofar as Whitehead is concerned. What is more, I am convinced that this line of approach is both right and true in a more general sense. Thus there is a definitely christological aspect at the heart of talk about the new model.

Having said that, however, it must also be noted that this christological aspect should not be understood as if it were exclusive. There is no christocentrism in it, when that word is used (as so often it has been used in theological circles) to make the event of Jesus Christ the *only* clue to deity and therefore to see him as an anomaly in the God-world relationship. As I have often urged in other writing about the significance of Jesus for Christian faith, he must be taken as the classical instance, the defining moment if you will, in that wider relationship, not as the absolutely unique and unparalleled moment, without prior intimations and therefore appearing as a bolt from the blue, unrelated to what has gone on before him and what has happened after him. If we are to use here the highly ambiguous word 'unique' in any meaningful sense, we must follow the usage of Professor C. F. D. Moule of Cambridge, who in commenting on the general New Testament view has spoken of Jesus' uniqueness as 'inclusive' rather than 'exclusive'. In my view the word 'unique' is unfortunate, however; and I should propose in its place such terms as the one already used above, definitive or defining, and such others as decisive, indicative, etc., all of which safeguard the speciality of the event – for like every event, the event of Christ has this quality, making it distinctive and particular – but also preserve the relational aspect of Christ to the wider activity of God in the world.

We shall be returning at the end of this chapter to some of the points made above. Now, however, it will be helpful if we look at the general biblical story and attempt to see its relevance to the model which I have proposed. For there can be no doubt that the new model is much closer to that biblical account (and to its portrayal of God) than was the old model. After all the Bible speaks always about God in relationship with his world; it says nothing about God's existing in separation or remoteness from that world. Whatever it has to tell us about God is always told in the light of, and as an implication drawn from, what the Jewish people believed they knew of God from his activity in the creation.

We shall not be able to understand properly what the biblical material tells us unless we accept without hesitation the type of biblical study which for the last hundred years has been carried on by experts in this field. If the Bible is read, as so often it is read in conservative religious circles and by the theologians who speak for such circles, as inerrant in every detail; if we assume that any portion of the Old Testament, for example, stands on precisely the same level, for our portrayal of deity, as every other passage; if we fail to grasp the way in which Jewish thinking about God developed from stage to stage in response to the experience of the Jewish people and the interpretation of that experience by their most discerning seers and sages – if we do this, we shall get the picture entirely wrong. Indeed the difficulty with the frequently used phrase 'The Word of God', when applied to the scriptures, is that it can and usually does suggest to the ordinary person that we are to take those scriptures as if they were dictated by God and that we must therefore accept each and every bit of material which they contain as being equally a 'message' from God to men. Yet our moral and rational understanding revolts at this levelling – even if it is called a levelling 'up' rather than 'down'. There may be a sense in which the term 'Word of God' is appropriate to scripture; but it would be much wiser and more intelligent, as well as more religiously helpful, if it were recognized that what we have in that varied collection of literary material is the words of men – or better phrased, what was believed by this or that person, in this or that place and time, and in this or that particular circumstance and situation, about what God was understood in some fashion to have revealed or disclosed. This delivers us from the tendency to adopt either old-fashioned fundamentalism, in which the scriptures are taken to be entirely inerrant in every detail; or the more modern variety of fundamentalism, in which it is assumed that there are clearly discernible motifs which run through the entire collection and which are present to some degree and in some fashion everywhere within it.

With so much said about approach, let us now attempt to sketch the way in which the biblical picture of God did in fact develop, with recognition of the many different stresses and with an awareness of the many backward moves which are quite as apparent as is the more general forward thrust from earliest days to the time of Jesus and his first disciples. In doing this, we must read the 'books' of the Bible in the order of their time of writing rather than in the order found in most printed editions, where we start with Genesis and end with Revelation and hence may very well assume (unless we are professional biblical scholars) that this is how we *ought* to read and interpret the material.

The first stage of Jewish history has been called by Old Testament scholars the period of primitive Yahwism. Yahweh, of course, is the word which means 'God', although it is not the only one found in the Jewish scriptures. What then was the nature of this very early Jewish outlook and how was deity pictured in it? What was the model after which those first Jews about whom we have historical information fashioned their understanding of God? I do not intend to burden these pages with biblical references to book, chapter, and verse; it will suffice to say that for any reader who lacks familiarity with the details of the scriptures, a study of such volumes as *The Jerome Biblical Commentary* (Chapman 1969) or *The Interpreter's Bible* (Abingdon 1977), especially the introductory essays in each of them, will provide adequate evidence for what is here being said.

The primitive Hebrews were a nomadic people, living in desert territory somewhere in the Arabian peninsula. They were exposed to all the perils which life in such a place would imply. Sudden storms with violent winds, in certain areas (like the Sinaitic peninsula into which eventually they wandered) volcanic eruption, possibly earthquakes, and the like would be familiar and terrifying. There was also the constant threat of conflict with other inhabitants of the region; the kind of warfare which would follow was devastating and frightful, with almost indiscriminate slaughter and with cruelty and torture. What was more, their means of livelihood were restricted to what was available to them in the places into which they wandered. They went from one area to another in that vast arid region, seeking for such pasture for their flocks as was available, looking for fertile oases where they might find refuge, and always with an existence which was in danger of attack from their enemies who also sought places and opportunities for pasture and food.

Religion for the primitive Hebrew tribes was evidently not dissimilar from that of their neighbours. Spirits dwelt in springs, at wells, and were also present at places which in one way or another were unusual or striking. Something of the same sort of religion is still to be found among Bedouins in the Arabian peninsula. But, as time went on, the Hebrew mind tended to unify these various spirits into one great and all-controlling power. The power was chiefly manifested in the unusual and extraordinary, and primarily in the release of force seen in storm, earthquake, volcanic eruption, or moments of battle; yet it was also active in whatever appeared to promote the welfare of the people who worshipped it. Traces of this sort of religious awareness are found scattered through the earliest written documents in the Old Testament, doubtless set down after decades of oral repetition.

And then something happened. It is not at all clear just what that something was, but traditionally it was associated with some of the Hebrew people who presumably had wandered into Egypt under pressure to find supplies. There they had been given the status of slaves, but at least they had some security of livelihood. However, the oppression under which they were living, possibly also the forced labour which was their lot, led some of them to rebel. Under a leader called Moses, about whom many stories – some doubtless legendary but others with an historical basis – were told in later years and incorporated into the sacred records of the Hebrew people, these Jews escaped from Egypt and for many years wandered about in what is now the Sinaitic peninsula and adjacent territory. This departure from Egypt was regarded by them as a great deliverance from oppression and was associated in their minds with their passage over a shallow inlet or marsh which they had managed to negotiate safely. The upshot of the whole series of events was the emergence of a new sort of certainty. The deity who previously had been manifested chiefly in catastrophic and destructive activity was now taken to be primarily concerned with the justice of the Jewish cause in escaping from 'captivity' in Egypt. According to the inherited tradition, the exponent of this newer conception was Moses. Very likely he was a man of unusual ability, a natural leader, and one who could also persuade various other related Jewish tribes who had not been in Egypt that they all belonged together to a common race of people. They were led to see that God had chosen them, had saved them, and had taken steps to lead them to a 'promised land' where they might dwell in peace and safety. So it came about that coercive power, hitherto known for the most part through extraordinary interventions in the affairs of nature and then in their own history, was now interpreted as power exercised for the cause of justice. This meant that the power known in such phenomena was essentially a 'power that made for righteousness' and was concerned above all to see that justice was done to the people he had chosen for himself. Other gods were not denied existence; but, compared to Yahweh, they were interested only in other peoples and certainly they were not supreme and all-controlling as was their own Jewish deity.

Eventually, through a series of raids and incursions, the Jewish tribes managed to gain increasing control of the land of Canaan. In that fertile territory there were already people who had settled there centuries before and who had developed their own culture, which was evidently more sophisticated than that of the intruding Hebrew tribes. In religious matters, the resident people worshipped local deities called baalim or 'lords'; these were supposed to dwell in high places and to be given honour by ceremonies held in such centres. The baalim were gods of fertility, both natural and human; they were believed to be interested in the cultivation of the land and in the promotion of prosperity for those who worshipped them. Inevitably, as time went on, the new occupants came to associate Yahweh with some of the attributes and interests of those whose control of the land had been taken from them by the invaders. So Yahweh was seen to be not only the power that made for righteousness and defended his own people; he was also the deity who cared for 'seed-time and harvest', for cultivation of the crops, for the orderly succession of the seasons, and for the natural environment in which his people now lived. As the assimilation went on, in early days and for many succeeding decades, perhaps even centuries, there was an inevitable conflict between the austerity of Yahweh and the more sensuous character of the older baalim. Eventually, however, under a series of early prophets or seers, Yahweh was recognized as supreme; the excesses, sexual and otherwise, of the baalim were attacked. Yahweh was now not only the special deity of the Hebrew people; he was also taken to be the 'Lord of lords', who was in control of all nature and all human life. In technical terms, the Jews slowly moved from henotheism, in which their God was one among many yet for them supreme over the many, to a monotheism in which there could be but one divine being.

But development did not stop at this point. Some of the prophets came to reflect deeply upon their own experience and the history of their people. Further, in their attempts to obey the commandments of Yahweh, they were brought to realize that there was a more personal relationship between the divine and human, in which Yahweh showed himself as a caring deity. He was faithful to his promises – after all they *had* occupied and gained control over Canaan. He was merciful, in that he had continually spared his people from the consequences of their wrong-doing and from the possibility of defeat and destruction. In relationship with him, there was a sense of abundant life or *shalom*, which included peace and security as well as deliverance from oppressors and enemy peoples.

Thus for the thoughtful and religiously-minded Jewish leaders, it was possible to see Yahweh as indeed supreme in power, but also as himself righteous and profoundly concerned for righteousness not only within the society of Jews but also among other peoples. More than that, he was one whose inner character could be indicated by the Hebrew word *chesed*, which means precisely loving-kindness, mercy, and gracious caring for his human children, even when they had disobeyed him and had sought their own way and will. This was a forgiving deity, prepared to accept any who turned to him in repentence for their wrong-doing. This was a personalized deity, appropriately thought of in terms of human experience, although immeasurably greater, utterly transcendent and beyond human comprehension. This was the 'high and lofty one who inhabits eternity, whose name is "holy" '; yet this was also the one who 'dwelt with those who are of a humble spirit'. This was a good, a righteous, and a loving deity, however stern might be his demands and however ready he might be to punish those who rejected his will and attempted to live apart from his ever-present action.

The Old Testament reaches its highest point, religiously speaking, in such prophetic figures as Isaiah, Hosea, Jeremiah, and the Second Isaiah (whose oracles are included in the later sections of the book called by the name of the 'first' prophet of that book). In these prophets, and more particularly in Hosea and Jeremiah, a further insight is found, which was not developed fully at the time but none the less was present and had promise of becoming central in the Jewish tradition. Whereas in the larger part of the prophetic tradition, and in the religion which was dependent upon that tradition (which, incidently, included much of the priestly side of Jewish life, a point often forgotten by Protestant biblical scholars who have sought to make a far too sharp contrast between the prophet and the priest), Yahweh was seen to be ready graciously to receive any who turned to him in repentence, there was now also a hint, and time and again much more than a hint, that Yahweh was the one who himself initiated that return. He could and he would seek for his own, even when they were far away from him in disobedience and revolt.

It is unfortunate that some Christian theologians have failed to see this note in late Jewish piety and hence have mistakenly claimed that in Jesus, and in him for the first time, there was to be found just such an emphasis on God as prevenient in his loving and outgoing in his concern to bring back those who had strayed. None the less, it *is* true that this emphasis was especially central to what Jesus, when he appeared and lived and taught, both acted upon and proclaimed. Years ago, the Jewish scholar Claude Montefiore admitted, not reluctantly but with vigour and strong conviction, that in this respect Jesus was not in contradiction to the Jewish tradition in which he had his place but rather was bringing that tradition to its most adequate and supreme expression.

For those Jews who first became followers of Jesus, the itinerant teacher from Nazareth, and later for the others who heard about him (including, of course, numbers of non-Jews in the Graeco-Roman world, as word about this Jesus was carried to them by early missionary figures), a new kind of faith was born. The New Testament is the witness to this faith. It tells about Jesus himself, through the gospel material which is a setting-down of the oral tradition which had grown up about him as he was remembered by those who had companied with him. It also includes the response which was made to him. The gospels themselves are written 'from faith to faith'. They are not biographical material in the sense in which we might write the life of somebody known to us, today. Rather, they are stories told about Jesus – his sayings and his doings – which inevitably reflect a response and witness to him made in just such faith. The rest of the New Testament, including the account of the first days of the Christian fellowship told in Acts and such writing as the letters of Paul, as well as material attributed to other early Christian spokesmen, reflects the development of faith in Jesus. But faith in him *as what*?

We can see the development of this faith in Jesus from the days when he was interpreted as 'a prophet like unto Moses', through the period when he was somehow seen as one chosen and anointed by God (hence 'Messiah', which means the 'anointed one'), to the time when he was given even more exalted status, so that he was somehow identified with the divine activity in the world and in history and hence could be regarded as himself in some sense divine – although precisely *how* that was to be stated, without diminishing the fact of his genuine humanity, was a matter for later generations to ponder. But the *what* about Jesus can be put concisely in this fashion: in this man, the seeking and enriching and redeeming love of God was taught in word and enacted in deed. To know Jesus, then, was to know God in his loving concern for his human children. It was to be given the assurance that whatever else could be said about deity, 'his nature and his name is Love', as Charles Wesley put it. Later terms and developed doctrinal definitions (like incarnation) are secondary to this experiential reality. They may, or they may not, be satisfactory to us today. Yet they are indicative of the significance which men and women then found and still continue to find in him. This now brings us to the specifically christological aspect as it is relevant to the new model for God.

The life of Jesus is an historical fact, known to us through the response made to it as witnessed in the New Testament. Whitehead once said, 'Buddhism and Christianity find their origins respectively in two inspired moments of history, the life of the Buddha and the life of Christ. The Buddha gave his doctrine to enlighten the world; Christ gave his life. It is for Christians to discern the doctrine.' And he went on to notice that while 'we do not possess a systematic detailed record of the life of Christ . . . we do possess a peculiarly vivid record of the first response to it in the minds of the first disciples after the lapse of some years, with their recollections, interpretations, and incipient formulations' (*Religion in the Making*, p. 55).

Now this life, said Whitehead, 'is not an exhibiting of over-ruling power. Its glory is for those who discern it . . . Its power lies in its absence of force. It has the decisiveness of a supreme ideal, and that is why the history of the world divides at this point of time.' (ibid., pp. 56–7) What is central to Christianity is Jesus grasped by the insight of the earliest Christians in their response to him in faith, and in the witness given by those who thus were grasped by him. All this is reflected for us in the New Testament records. The Christian believes that 'by appeal to the direct intuition of special occasions' – in this case the 'special occasion' of Jesus – there is given a clue which is of 'universal validity, to be applied by faith to the ordering of all occasions' (ibid., p. 31). This point, already indicated in our earlier discussion, cannot be over-estimated.

The Christian conviction has been formulated in theological idiom, to be sure. But what is significant for us is not the details of the formulations nor even the formulations themselves, but the reality with which they deal. Theological definition and formulation, what- ever it may be, is inevitably tied in with the philosophy which it presupposes. Hence, again in Whitehead's words, 'a dogma' – in the sense of a precise formulation – 'can never be final; it can only be adequate' to the period in which it was worked out. On the other hand, 'the great instantaneous conviction' behind the dogma is the gospel or good news; and Christian experience through the ages has been enabled to 'maintain its identity by its recurrence to the inspired simplicity of its origin' (ibid., p. 133).

The Christian fellowship is the community in which this process of development, along with the recurrent appeal to the 'originating moment' has taken place. Religious faith is dependent upon specific human confrontation with 'what is permanent in the nature of things'; and hence it has about it, obviously enough, a certain quality of 'solitariness', which means, not the isolation or separation of one human being from other human beings, but a direct relevance and significance for each believer. Whitehead's meaning here can only be grasped when we have seen that for him 'there is no such thing as absolute solitariness' since 'each entity requires its environment' and therefore 'man cannot seclude himself from society' (ibid., p. 132). On the one hand, there must be personal appropriation through which faith works by 'cleansing the inward parts'; on the other hand, there must be social belonging because religion has 'for its topic the individual in community'.

The biblical aspect, so central to the new model, is essentially an appeal to the event in history from which the Christian community took its rise: namely, Jesus Christ, understood as a concrete event which includes what went before to prepare for his appearing, the way in which he was received and understood in the response made to him in the earliest days, and what has happened in consequence of his coming. The event includes all this. Like every other occurrence, it brings to a focus the past which is inherited and then used, the present in which decision is made, and the consequences which are the result of such decisions. In this sense the event of Christ, once more in Whitehead's words (*Adventures of Ideas*, p. 170), is 'the supreme moment in history, according to the Christian religion'. Whitehead goes on to describe this in beautiful and moving language:

> The essence of Christianity is the appeal to the life of Christ as a revelation of the nature of God and of his agency in the world. The record is fragmentary, inconsistent, and uncertain . . . But there can be no doubt as to what elements in the record have evoked a response from all that is best in human nature. The Mother, the Child, and the bare manger: the lowly man, homeless and self-forgetful, with his message of peace, love, and sympathy: the suffering, the agony, the tender words as life ebbed, the final despair: and the whole with the authority of supreme victory . . .

Can there be any doubt that the power of Christianity lies in its revelation in act of that which Plato divined in theory?

What *did* Plato thus divine 'in theory'? Surely it was what White-head, in the same passage, puts in these words: 'The divine element in the world is to be conceived as a persuasive agency and not as a coercive agency.' So we are brought back to the affirmation that God is essentially nothing other than Love, the cosmic Lover, known to be this not so much through human theorizing or speculation – important as these may be – but rather through historical actuality. 'For God so loved the world that he gave . . .' as we read in St John's Gospel; and again, in the First Epistle of St John, 'Herein is love, not that we loved God but that he loved us, and sent his Son that we might live through him'. In a later chapter I shall make some suggestions about how this christological position may be stated in our own time.

In presenting the new model, I urged that this affirmation of divine Love is the basic criterion by which anything and everything that is said about God must be judged. What is said about God, yes; but also what is said about the world and about human existence in relationship with God must be evaluated by the degree to which such statements are in conformity with the affirmation that God is Love. A statement which cannot be reconciled with that affirmation, or which in some fashion minimizes or radically modifies it, must be rejected; it can have no place in a proper Christian understanding of God. Judged by that criterion, it is plain enough that a good deal of conventional theology, above all in its talk about God, like much in conventional forms of worship and in conventional moral teaching, has no ultimate claim upon our allegiance. The criterion obliges us to think through once again what it means to 'have faith in God' and what it means to profess the Christian faith itself; and therefore to be bold enough to undertake a radical revision of our theology, our liturgy, our personal devotion, and our notions of morality.

The end result will be a more profoundly biblical understanding, provided we interpret the Bible in the light of our best modern knowledge of its contents and how they came to be set down. We shall be able to grasp the thrilling fact that the whole story of creation is a cosmic adventure in what Teilhard de Chardin called 'amoriza-tion' (as we have noted). Our human vocation and destiny is to be 'co-creators' or 'fellow-workers' with the cosmic Lover who is God; and we ourselves shall be appraised by our glad and willing sharing, or failure to share, in that great adventure. All this, to my mind, is entailed once we have adopted for ourselves the 'Galilean' model of God.

7

Cosmic Love and the Fact of Evil

The title of this chapter does not speak of 'the problem of evil' but of the *fact* of evil. Two comments are appropriate in this connection. First, that I have put together, in one bag, so to say, a number of different things which are commonly described as evil. Hence I must unpack the bag and consider the variety of evils in our experience with the genuine distinctions among them that must be made in this respect. Second, by refusing to call evil or evils a 'problem', I am trying to indicate that many of those things which we mean when using that word 'evil' (either in the singular or in the plural) are simply *given* – they are tied in with the freedom of created occasions and their capacity to bring about certain consequences. They are not to be regarded as willed by God in a direct fashion, nor as if they were 'permitted' by God although things might have been otherwise. Evil as a 'problem' suggests a view of God, a model for our apprehending God, which in this book we have rejected altogether: that is to say, a portrayal of God as all-controlling, totally omnipotent, responsible for whatever happens just as it happens. But with the model of God that this book presents and defends, nothing of the sort can be asserted.

Although for convenience I have used the word 'evil' in the singular in giving a title to this chapter, I am convinced that to lump together a great number of quite different facts suggests a confusion of understanding. In truth, there are several sorts of thing which we usually tend to classify as being evil; and failure to recognize the differences may lead us to seek for a solution which will seem to cover all these without our looking squarely at each in its own distinctive quality. Hence I shall now direct attention to the variety of evils in our experience. I shall endeavour to show that when these are properly described, so far as we are able to do so, and when our model of God is the one for which I have argued in earlier chapters, we find ourselves looking at a world which is not properly styled 'the best of all possible worlds', in the sense of 'the best conceivable', but yet which is not to be seen as a world concerning which there can only be unmitigated pessimism. I wish to urge that the world which we know is such that neither an easy optimism nor a facile pessimism are possible positions, but rather a genuine *realism*, which will require (of course), what Thomas Hardy once called 'a full look at the worst'. At the same time I shall urge that there can be an *ultimate* optimism, once we have correctly understood God's relationship to the creation. This ultimate optimism will be reached only through honest acceptance of the tragic element both in our own experience and in the divine Love that is the chief causative agency, but not the only such agency – and also the final receptive agency. A fuller discussion of this will be found in my *Cosmic Love and Human Wrong* (Paulist Press 1978).

First, let us consider the variety of situations or occasions which we commonly describe by the word 'evil'. Obviously I am here assuming, as I have done throughout this book, that ours is a world of change and development, not a static and fixed order. Hence I take for granted that the components of the world are not things or substances, but events, happenings, or occurrences – 'energy-events', in John Hick's phrase. Further, I take for granted that this is a societal world, in which each event is affected by and affects every other event. In that world the strongest power is not coercive force but persuasive or luring action, appropriately called in theistic discourse the 'divine Love'; this Love is indeed God, as the chief causative agency and the final receptive agency. In that context and with those presuppositions we can make significant distinctions among the various evils with which we are familiar.

Thus there are the disorders which we observe in the so-called natural world: earthquakes, volcanic eruptions, hurricanes, tidal waves, and the like. As a matter of fact, nobody would think of calling these evil until or unless there is some sort of life, usually human life, which is imperilled, damaged, or destroyed through their happening. What is more, anyone who has read L. J. Henderson's classic work *The Fitness of the Environment*, published many years ago, or similar studies of the relation of the natural order to the possibility of the existence of living beings, knows that for the most part such disorders are tied in with the sort of world in which we live and that without their occurring that possibility of life would be ruled out of the picture. The givenness of a creation like the one we inhabit is marked by phenomena which make life possible by maintaining the proper physical and chemical conditions, by keeping gradations of heat and cold within suitable limits, and by an adjustment and ordering that preserve a viable environment for animate creatures including man. At this point, of course, we also face the enormous damage which our own human activity has inflicted on that natural order, thanks to our violation of what is nowadays called 'the ecological balance' and hence bringing about consequences whose seriousness is more and more apparent. But this last consideration belongs to a later point in this chapter.

Unless it could be shown that the regularities which are found in the natural order and the repeated patterns which manifest themselves to the student of that order are alterable without undoing the whole cosmic enterprise, we have every right to conclude that the way things happen at that level cannot be changed nor can the consequences be prevented. It is indeed a *given*. We might even say that it is a 'must' if there is to be a creation at all which can eventually produce, and provide a setting for, the 'higher' types of existence. Otherwise we should not have those more complicated patterns of energy-events which are animate, possessed of some degree of responsible freedom, and at some levels are conscious and self-conscious. There is no reason to see in natural disasters like those we have mentioned the peculiarly direct activity of God, after the fashion of the insurance policy's phrase 'acts of God'. There is no reason to assume that an occurrence in which human activity is not observed must be divinely willed, purposed, and performed.

On the other hand, if God is not the arbitrary creator of the world and its ruler in that autocratic sense, but rather is 'with his creation', moulding it from everlasting to everlasting and always working in, with, and through *some* created state of affairs, there is no necessary problem here. Rather, there is the plain fact of natural occurrences which under certain circumstances we humans tend to describe as evil. There is sufficient independence in the created order for it to 'make itself'; and there is also sufficient continuity to ensure that it shall be a cosmos and not sheer chaos. Exercise of divine power as persuasive Love does not negate that independence, nor does it deny the continuity which observation discloses. Rather, it both accepts that independence and uses it towards the emergence of novelty, while it also employs a limited coercive pressure to preserve continuity and prevent orderly advance from degenerating into meaningless anarchy.

Here I must introduce a brief discussion to show that the notion of a 'before creation', when God existed entirely alone in majestic isolation from some world in which he might creatively work, seems a bit of cosmological nonsense that ought to be dismissed for the absurdity that it is. Nor am I alone in thinking so. For even in the scholastic theology of the Middle Ages, the doctrine of creation was not a doctrine of supposed 'absolute beginnings', but a doctrine having to do with the dependence of creation on God. It was a way of saying that apart from God's action within the creation, that creation would collapse into nothingness.

I am glad to be able to refer here to some comments which were made a few years ago by the English theologian F. W. Dillistone. He remarked that there was no philosophical or theological reason to rule out the possibility that throughout all time there had been some creative possibility, some primordial stuff upon which the divine activity might work. While always dependent upon God in its prior states for its continuance, this could well be in one sense coeval with him. As in the Genesis creation myth, biblical talk about some aboriginal chaos might very well be interpreted as a poetic statement of an early Hebrew insight which refused ever to think of God as without a world. Questions about beginnings, in the usual meaning of that word, would remain a matter for scientific discussion, based upon scientific knowledge; they would be cosmological in that sense. But they would not be theologically significant. God is the one *final* dependability, just as he is the chief causal agency in what goes on, the lure towards realization of novelty, the guarantor of a basic pattern or order, and the final recipient of what is accomplished in the world. Dr Dillistone makes this clear when he writes as follows:

> It is possible to suggest that the word 'create' as used by the Bible was an artistic rather than a scientific word, and that its use by scientists has not served the interests of clarification. If, however, the precise scientific reference is omitted it then becomes possible to imagine the universe as a meaningful whole and as the work of a personal mind shaping available materials. Whence the materials come, the Bible does not enquire. That a formless concentration of energy might have existed with God before the creation of the world does not seem to me an impossible conception to entertain (*The Christian Faith*, Hodder and Stoughton 1964).

Following this line of thought, we may say that God works with a 'formless creation of energy' and from it brings into existence new and significant occasions through which his creative purpose can be expressed. This 'concentration' exists not *before* creation, since that would suggest a time when God as creator did not have a creation, but rather exists as ceaselessly providing for him, at all times and places, the continuing material with which he works as he acts to bring into existence the opportunities in which his goodness or love may be expressed. We know nothing at all of a *before* or *after* creation, in any literal temporal sense of the words; we know only the creation as it now presents itself to us and in which we live. By faith we also know of the cosmic Love that works creatively in the world. Thus talk of before and after is mythological; it is a way of saying something about what God is always up to, in himself and in respect to his purpose for the world, as well as in the realization of that purpose through the creation of which we are a part.

Reading the Bible as if it were a scientific manual or a literal historical record leads us astray. The Genesis story is what we have just said it is: a way of affirming God's boundless creativity, his utter supremacy, and the ultimate dependence of all things upon his creative action. Read in that fashion, the Genesis story does not contradict the point which Dr Dillistone was making. Even Aquinas found nothing intrinsically wrong in the notion that God eternally creates the world. It was only because he believed, as did everyone in his age, that the creation story in Genesis must be taken in a literal historical sense, that he felt obliged to say that this creation had a 'temporal beginning'. Since *we* do not take the Genesis material in that fashion, we have no reason to reject the view that God *and* the world are always there, and there together, although we must accept the status of the world in its present patterning as dependent upon God for the goods which are being accomplished in it.

Creation, then, need not mean that first there was quite literally nothing at all and then a split-second later there was a world. Even the doctrine that God creates *ex nihilo* (out of nothing) need not be interpreted in that wooden and simple-minded way. It can and should mean that from among the range of possibilities and by the use of the materials which antecedent events have already moulded, God brings into existence something that as an emergent is genuinely new, yet is in continuity with what had gone before and with the total process of creative advance. The genuinely new is a configuration, a constella-tion, a focusing, in an entity with its initial aim, its potentialities, its capacity for decision, its opportunity to actualize and hence bring to fulfilment what God purposes – but with opportunity also, by the same capacity for decision, to fail to do this. The word 'nothing' in this context need not signify some hypothetically absolute *nihil*, but simply the absence of that particular occasion with its potentialities.

We now proceed with our consideration of things that we call evil. We know very well that there is suffering and pain at the level of sentient existence, whether this is less developed biological life or more sophisticated animal or human existence. We should not commit here the 'pathetic fallacy' and assume that, say, a crab whose claw has been torn off in a struggle with another crab has the same sensitivity that we should have if an arm or leg were wrenched from our body. There are degrees of sensitivity; and the higher the organism is in its nervous systems, the more affected will be its feeling of pain. I am not urging a callous approach; I am only warning against the sentimentality which carries to a preposterous extreme the compassion we ought to feel about all suffering however slight or insignificant it may be. Furthermore, the development of physiological science has made it clear that the nervous systems which make pain possible also make pleasure possible. We cannot have the opportunity of experiencing the latter without the chance of experiencing the former. This we known in our own existence as humans. Certainly the same point may be made, with appropriate qualifications, at levels below the human. In this sense, then, I suggest that the word 'evil' may very well be misapplied in this connection.

But there is a point where it seems more appropriate. When cancer cells proliferate, without regard for their host, so that they exercise a highly damaging effect on that host, then surely we may say that we are in the presence of what constitutes, in that context, something decidely evil. For wherever there is some analogue, however faint, to entirely self-assertive activity, there is the denial of harmony and cooperation. Some of the countless actual entities in the creation, in moving towards the realization of their proper aim, can and do pay no attention to the pattern of commonalty or sociality. Since each energy-event has its own degree of power and its own capacity for causal activity, and since each such entity naturally seeks its own intensity of realization, it may very well act in a fashion that disregards the wider shared good. This is evil because it prevents the coming into existence of just such a socially shared way of becoming. And here we may say that God's action in the creation is exercised in working to avoid such conflict as will destroy enriching contrast; God will always maintain some genuine order that calls a halt to movements towards sheer and unrelieved disorder, in chaos or anarchy.

We come next to the level of psychological or emotional anguish. 'We look before and after/And pine for what is not': so says the poet.

We suffer emotionally and mentally, both for ourselves and for others; and they suffer in the same way. Yet here we have the inevitable concomitant of our experiencing joy, elation, and pleasure. We have also the reality of our sociality, our influencing and being influenced by others. This shows itself when we 'rejoice with them that do rejoice, and weep with them that do weep'. With a congeries of innumerable centres of activity, some will fail to achieve their proper self-actualization; some will refuse (whether in a highly conscious or in a vague manner) to act in harmony with their fellows in the total creative advance. Often the consequences are tragic, as we well know.

Finally we are aware of moral evil. We see *wilfully* chosen self-assertion, *wilful* failure to move forward along the line of advance towards harmonious existence, *wilful* rejection of lures that have been offered for the more adequate social realization of potentiality. Responsibility rests here with the agencies which thus 'decide' by cutting off *this* through accepting *that*. Such responsibility presupposes a freedom which runs through the whole creation and reaches its fullest expression, so far as we are aware, at the level of human choice among relevant possibilities. Freedom in this sense entails accountability for the use to which it is put. However much our free decisions may be limited or distorted by circumstance, situation, heredity, and environmental pressure, there is in all human experience an awareness that such freedom is indelibly ours, along with the accountability which follows from it.

Religious people speak of sin and rightly regard this as evil. But we must ask what we mean by 'sin'. In the perspective taken in this book, the answer is plain enough. Sin in any significant religious sense is not the violation of imposed rules or commandments which have arbitrarily been imposed upon us. Rather, it is the wilful breaking of relationships between ourselves and the creative and receptive Love that is God. It is also the wilful breaking of intentional loving and just relationships with our fellows. It is the rejection of love on the creaturely level, which has its corollary in the rejection of the divine Love that seeks to work through our human endeavour. This certainly is a very evil thing; and we need have no hesitation in calling it just that.

We have now considered a variety of 'wrongs' – failure to advance, backwaters in the creative process, refusal of cooperation and harmonious development, and false self-centeredness. The cosmos is indeed best interpreted as tragic: there is no place for a proximate optimism about the world which we know. A realistic appraisal of that world forces us to recognize and accept the fact that there is much in it that is appalling, terrifying, horrible – yes, evil – at different levels and in different modes. What Miguel de Unamuno styled 'the tragic sense of life' cannot be avoided by any civilized human being. There must be what we might call a *provisional* pessimism in respect to the state of affairs in which we are immersed and in which we play our own part. We are all caught in this situation, since we are 'members one of another' in a societal world. This is patently true at the human level. It has its ramifications elsewhere in the animal realm as a given fact; and it is also manifested in our wilful aggression against the natural order.

We have said that in a processive world, whose constituents are countless actual entities which each have power, freedom, capacity for decision, and with all the risk or 'chanciness' that is involved, the chief causative agency is God. But we have also insisted that God does not possess *all* causative responsibility. There are the other entities, each of them with its own causal efficacy. Since our model for God is sheer Love, the divine causation cannot be seen as omnipotence in the sense of absolute over-riding of all those other agencies. On the contrary the world's 'set-up' is such that all entities may and do exercise their own causal potency. God respects and does not negate this. Indeed in such a set-up he cannot, without contradicting the way in which things function; and as Peter Hamilton has well said, God always 'keeps the rules'. Certainly he labours ceaselessly to persuade every creaturely agent to act in such a fashion that it will actualize its possibility and realize its aim, in harmonious solidarity with others. But even so, God can be frustrated in his concrete working by the order in which he is active. His frustration may be but temporary; and there may be a conclusion of the matter which contributes to his own enjoyment and to the best good of the creatures. But we should also recognize that in the world we know limits have been established to prevent enriching contrast from becoming destructive conflict which will end in chaotic anarchy. God does not function as primary coercive drive which has its way regardless of everything else in the world. He is Love; his working is towards what, as we have seen, Teilhard de Chardin called 'amorization'. But that means that there are limitations with which he must reckon.

If to some readers this seems to point to what is sometimes styled a finite God, the answer is that such a characterization is inaccurate and entirely misleading. This error arises because it wrongly portrays God as if he could have the possibility of exerting totally omnipotent control and hence deny his own loving nature. It suggests that he does not exemplify in an eminent fashion the very categories which of necessity apply to any and every actuality. Far from being finite, in a pejorative sense, God is infinite in his Love, his goodness, his inexhaustible readiness to lure, win, persuade, and invite response. Only those who are enamoured of force in its coercive sense could consider this model to be a denial of God's *proper* infinity. The charge, a finite God, is a red-herring and need not worry us.

There is something more to be said. In the perspective of Process Thought adopted in this book, God is from everlasting to everlasting. He is not eternal *if* that is taken to suggest that he is entirely above and beyond all succession and without any participation in historical movement. But God is eminently temporal. This is to say that with a past from which he *is* and with which he has worked, through a present in which he also *is* and through which he works, towards a future where he *will be* and where he will continue to work, time is real to him and in him. He is no *nunc stans*, in whom everything is already simultaneously present and done. Obviously his manner of being 'historical' must far exceed our limited and partial experience of the time-series; yet he is *in* history and history is *in* him. So we may say that God has 'all time in which to accomplish his purpose of love'. We may say even more than that, for God is the chief recipient of what has been accomplished in the world. We have already noted this when we spoke of the new model for God; but here we may develop the theme a bit more.

God receives into himself, and uses for further activity in the creation, whatever in that creation has been 'determined, dared, and done'. The di-polar picture of God, as supreme causative agency and supreme recipient; the model which sees God as primordial and consequent, in Whitehead's way of putting it; the understanding of God as both abstractly conceivable and concretely actual and operative, as Charles Hartshorne would phrase it: all this guarantees that his provision of initial aims and his luring of creaturely entities to achieve such aims is complemented by his 'saving everything that can be saved'. Since this is the case, there is room for what I have styled *ultimate* optimism, although even this must have a tragic quality. We need not assume that we ourselves will necessarily be aware, here or hereafter, that this victory occurs. The point is rather that all can be seen as making its contribution *ad maiorem dei gloriam* (to God's greater glory) – provided we recognize that *God's* glory is not the exhibition of worldly majesty nor coercive control, but the sharing of his Love in 'widest commonalty'. For the creature to have made a contribution to that Love, to have shared in it, to have had defects and distortions corrected by it, and to have been received into it, is or ought to be sufficient.

What have such considerations got to do with the fact of evil, in all its forms, in the world we know? To my mind the answer is that the created entities in the world are called to be 'co-creators' with God – 'fellow-workers', as St Paul put it. Working with God who is Love, in his eager and indefatigable concern for establishing good over bad, care over indifference, justice over injustice and oppression, and love over hatred, we can face up to the evils which we recognize and experience, and can ourselves be 'more than conquerors through him who loved us'. A Christian will see this placarded before him in Jesus Christ, defeated on the Cross yet in that very defeat victorious. For the Christian, Good Friday is suffused with the light of Easter morning. What Jesus is, what Jesus did, and what Jesus represents are everlastingly present in the consequent nature of God – in God as affected by the creation. Because this is so, the event of Christ provides for God new opportunities to work lovingly in the creation as in his 'superjective' aspect he thrusts back into the creation the achievement of Love crucified. This is what God is; this is what God is up to in the world.

The multiplicity of creative agents in a world in process makes evil, in its various forms and in all its horror, practically inevitable. Randolph Crump Miller has said in his admirable *American Spirit in Theology* (Pilgrim Press 1974, p. 171) that 'only through the same multiplicity could good become' a possibility and an actuality. When such good *is* accomplished, it is never lost. Whitehead said:

> For the perfected actuality, what is done in the world is transformed into a reality in heaven, and the reality in heaven passes back into the world. By reason of this reciprocal relation, the love in the world passes into the love in heaven, and floods back into the world. In this sense, God is the great companion – the fellow-sufferer who understands (*Process and Reality*, p. 532).

My final comment in this chapter is by way of a response to an acquaintance who had read an earlier draft of this book. He told me that to his mind such an approach to evil in all its forms was what he called 'a trivialization' which reduced evil, and more particularly human sin, to nothing more than 'backward drags, dangerous side-paths, and plain distortions'. For him and, he said, for most thoughtful people – although how he knew this I cannot see! – evil is 'radical'; it is 'rooted in the very nature of things'. Much the same criticism, it may be observed, was once made of Teilhard de Chardin's views, in a *monitum* issued from the Holy Office in Rome.

But I think that what we have here is a confusion of the evils we experience, as of the sin which we know all too well, with certain traditional descriptions or definitions. It is assumed that to speak differently is in effect to deny the reality and seriousness of those evils and that sin. I hope, however, that I have made it clear that I see all evils, and particularly moral evil and sin, as serious and tragic, as frighteningly prevalent, as making impossible any rosy optimistic view of the world or of human existence. Yet I reject any talk about such things as 'radical', if that word is taken in its proper dictionary meaning – namely, 'at the root of things'. If we speak in that fashion, we are denying outright the great Jewish and Christian affirmation of the essential goodness of the created order despite its patent distortion. We are impugning God himself. The evils and sin in the world, which we know so well and whose horror we feel so strongly, are defects in that good creation. They are existentially real and horrible. But they are not of the essence of creation itself. I do not see how we can think that they are, unless we are prepared also to subscribe to a manichean denigration of the creation and hence to deny the 'unity' of the divine reality we call God.

8

Loving Activity at Work in the World

The new model of God with which this book is concerned is essentially derived from loving activity in the world we know, and supremely as expressed in the life of Jesus Christ. As we shall be arguing later, it is appropriate and helpful to speak of God as the cosmic Lover, the phrase I have already used, because such a picture stresses the personal relationship which in religious life is enjoyed between that loving activity we call God, that basic thrust and drive in the cosmos whose quality is Love, and those who open themselves to it. But once more, however, we need to be sure that when we speak so strongly of love we understand that we are not using a word which suggests weakness, sentimentality, or undemanding toleration of anything and everything.

I wish therefore to give further meaning to the word 'love' by engaging very briefly in what might be called a phenomenological description of its workings in human experience.

To begin with, love is *commitment*. It is a concern for others which regards them as worthy of care and attention, although they may not seem at first sight to be anything of the sort. To love is to give; and above all it is to give oneself, to engage oneself with and on behalf of those with whom one is in contact, whether directly and immediately, or more remotely through report or some other means of communication.

In the second place, love is *mutuality*. That is to say, it is a generous giving and a gracious readiness to receive – hence it is a matter of shared life or a participation one in another or in others. Without such sharing we have only detached interest, without the warmth which comes from a genuine readiness to be open to the other in the relationship.

Thirdly, love is *fidelity*. It includes the intention of permanence in relationship. The lover of another sometimes says, 'This is for ever . . .'. And although it is quite likely that the 'for ever' may turn out not to be the case, the intention which is found in that phrase is somehow basic to loving and represents the deep desire of the one who utters it.

In the fourth place, love is *hopefulness*. By hopefulness here I do not mean a wistful desire that this or that good thing may happen; rather, I am speaking of what Baron Friedrich von Hügel once called, in a telling phrase, 'eager tiptoe expectancy'. That attitude which looks for the best that can be brought about in the one loved, is willing to do everything possible to promote good, to awaken the latent possibilities for it, and to assist in its growth and fruition.

Finally, love is *desired union*. Union is not loss of personal identity between persons loving and loved. It is a bringing together of two who by their commitment, sharing, faithfulness, and hope are enabled to enjoy life. A better word, perhaps, would have been *communion* since that may more readily denote two who are at one, rather than the situation in which there is loss of selfhood by submersion of one in the other.

Now all these seek to establish *fulfilment*, in which the possibility of human existence in concord, unity, harmony and cooperative enterprise is realized to a greater or lesser degree. To live in love is to know the greatest of all joys. It is also to know the anguish or suffering which often, perhaps always, accompanies genuine loving. This anguish or suffering is inevitable because of failure on both sides to actualize all that is desired and intended. What is more, precisely because *two* are here present, and each of the two has his or her own identity and integrity, there is between them 'the unplumbed, salt, estranging sea' of which Matthew Arnold once spoke. Not only physical separation but inability to enter completely into the deepest thought, intentions, desires, aspirations, pains, and failures of the other bring about a 'sorrow' which accompanies loving even at its best. The Italian word *dolore* is admirable in indicating this, for that word means not only pain but also sorrow, not only distress but also anguish. Yet no human lover would wish to be without such *dolore*, if its abolition were at the cost of not sharing the experience of love.

Love is like that when at its best and most compelling. But it is also *creative* since it enables the lover to think and do what may seem impossible, to achieve the incredibly difficult, and to achieve almost *de novo*, out of what 'appears' as nothing, things that are splendid and beautiful or that have at least the potentiality of becoming such.

Earlier I quoted the words of John Cobb and David Griffin about God as creative and responsive love. The creative side is accompanied by the responsive side. Love 'answers back'; it does not remain aloof and unconcerned; it cares, and it cares very deeply. So we have a model of God as a loving activity, in which there is from the divine side, and towards created entities, a commitment of himself; the establishment of mutuality or a two-sided relationship with these created entities, in which there is giving and receiving; an utter faithfulness in that this divine Love never forsakes the other but holds on through good and ill – it is the 'Love that will not let me go', as the hymn puts it; hopefulness with its eager and concerned readiness to work for the best good of the creature and with the expectation that such good will come into existence; and union or communion in which, without ever ceasing to be itself, the divine reality identifies itself with the other in a relationship which cannot be broken, no matter how much the loved one may stray from the right path. All this is for the fulfilment of cosmic Love, as well as for the realization of the potentiality of the created entity. It is not for the greater glory of God if by that we signify majestic self-assertion for its own sake; but certainly it is for that greater glory if by the phrase we mean the widest conceivable participation in a common life in which there is the joy of partnership in a shared enterprise.

So much, then, for what I have called a phenomenology of love, especially divine Love but also (and by derivation) the intention hidden in human love. This will enable us to talk in another chapter about the view of human nature which is implicit in such a model for deity.

The divine Love is at work in the world. What are the aspects or modes of such working that are relevant to the fulfilment of the divine intention for the widest and most complete sharing in a loving relationship, from which each receives enhanced delight even while each must know the anguish which is part of love's reality? ·

I think that we may speak of six aspects of this working in the world. They are (1) ordering, (2) initiating, (3) luring, (4) receiving, (5) responding, and (6) harmonizing. We shall consider them in that order. But first I suggest that we need to have an analogy for our thinking about God's relationship with the world, in addition to that which can be drawn from lover and beloved. The one that is most appropriate and useful is the relationship of mind and body as we know this in our human experience. Professor Charles Hartshorne has often written along these lines; but for a statement of the analogy

from an older thinker – and perhaps oddly, a famous defender of the
old model for deity – we may recall what St Thomas Aquinas said in
one place: 'In his rule God stands in relation to the whole universe as
the soul stands in relation to the body' (*II Sent*. 17. q.1, ad 1.).
Thomas here speaks of God's *rule*, by which he intends God's manner
of controlling the creation. He also says 'soul'. I propose that we
extend the analogy to cover the totality of the divine relationship
with the created world; and that we substitute 'mind' for 'soul', since
the exact meaning of the latter word is not clear. What then emerges
is the assertion that the divine reality 'stands' to the created world as
the human mind stands to the human body. In our human experience,
our bodily activity is influenced by, and acts in response to, the
thoughts which are ours, the intentions which we have, the purposes
which we would carry out, and the desired expression of such
thoughts, purposes, and intentions in some concrete behaviour.
Similarly, God influences the world, God acts in the world, and God
accomplishes his intentions in the world. The mind does not coerce
the body but patiently yet firmly 'persuades' the body. It pervades the
body yet it is not identical with the body. So also with God and the
world. The analogy is imperfect, like all analogies; but I believe it is
much less likely to mislead us than is the more familiar analogy of a
monarch ruling his subjects by force and hence coercing them to carry
out his will.

This analogy does not lead to a pantheistic identification of deity
and creation, yet it does require us to think of the two as very
intimately related and in real association one with the other in a
common enterprise. That enterprise, I have already said, is 'amorization', in the word used by Teilhard de Chardin. It has to do with
actualizing more love in the world, with augmenting the expression
of the divine Love, and with enabling the expression of human loving.
As to the actual relationship of God and world which it suggests, this
is along the lines of pan*en*theism. That word was first employed in
the nineteenth century by the German philosopher K. C. Krause
(whose dates are 1781–1832); it was also used by Baron von Hügel,
the Anglo-Austrian thinker whose writing was influential in the early
decades of this century. Panentheism has been defined as 'the belief
that the being of God includes and penetrates the whole universe, so
that every part of it exists in him, but (as against pantheism) that his
being is more than, and is not exhausted by, the universe' (*Oxford
Dictionary of the Christian Church*, ed. Cross & Livingstone, OUP
1974, p. 1027).

Granted some such conception, we are now ready to see that God
acts in the world, *first of all*, by ordering it according to a certain

pattern. I have said that the question which is often asked, 'When did the creation first come into being, so that it could be thus ordered?' seems to me a question that cannot be answered, for the simple reason that it presupposes a creator who does not 'have' a creation at some supposed moment prior to the temporal order and who then, for his own reasons, brings a creation into existence *ex nihilo*. I am sure that this is to talk linguistic nonsense. It is also to engage in the kind of speculation which was found in the older type of metaphysics and which presumed to theorize about absolute beginnings in a way that had no foundation in the world which we both experience and observe. Much better is acceptance of the belief that God and world are mutually implicated; and then to ask what the former is 'doing' in the latter.

I have said that what God is doing, in the first instance, is ordering the world. By this I mean that God is establishing the broad lines along which what might have been a chaotic or anarchic series of events is in fact maintained as a cosmos, in which there are 'rules' that are kept by all who, and by all that which, appears within it. There is a 'ground-plan', a 'creative advance' in Whitehead's phrase, which is inescapable and by which both God and the world operate. There is a creativity, or a possibility for the actualization of potentiality, which is basic to the entire enterprise. Without this there could not be a world of the sort which we recognize as being the case. Such ordering provides a general, over-all, continuity.

In the second place, the divine loving activity initiates novelty in the world. Within the wider continuity, there is room for the emergence of what is genuinely new, although this does not come about through intrusive or interruptive entrance from outside. Rather, it comes about by introduction of an aim or objective such as shall result in a modification of patterning; what went before now acquires different qualities or characteristics. Life emerges from inanimate existence; consciousness from living existence; self-awareness from conscious living existence. Experience is wider and more primordial than consciousness, which is supervenient upon it but not its contradiction. Human conscious experience is related with and emergent from animal existence; but it is not the same as animal existence, because it has its own peculiar characteristics which are irreducible to anything that happened prior to its appearance.

In each event, there is the 'material' which the past provides, and hence continuity; but there is also the particular potentiality which that event possesses. This is not something 'added on' to what has gone before, as if there were first the event and then an aim which was potential for it. The event appears and with it there appears the new potentiality; they are simultaneous and inseparable. Where does that novelty of aim or goal come from? In the model which I am proposing it is by God's working. Where such a divine working is not in some fashion operative, there could be only repetition of what has antecedently been the case.

Despite the attempt of Professor Donald Sherburne to show that the world in and of itself could provide such novelty of aim (he urges this in his essay on 'Whitehead without God' included in the symposium *Process Philosophy and Christian Thought*, pp. 305 ff.), I am convinced that such a view cannot be defended. On the contrary, I should say that without the introduction of novelty by the divine drive in the cosmos, the high likelihood would be only a 'uniformitarian world', which would resemble the nineteenth century idea of the reshuffling of already existent entities and not the real world which we know and about which contemporary science speaks – a world with freshness, vividness, difference, and risk.

In the third place, God does not only provide an initiating aim; he also works towards the achievement of that aim by each occasion. As the created entity is led to adopt for itself the aim which has been given it, so also it is lured or invited to move towards actualizing it. The aim has now become what in Process Thought is called 'the subjective aim'. It is the accepted concrete possibility, or better perhaps the 'ideal' possibility which is to be concretely realized, thus 'satisfying' or bringing to completion the potentiality of the event. Force is not used, but great persuasion is exercised to accomplish this, largely through the lures which, by prehension or grasping from the other affective entities, can be brought to bear upon this or that given occasion.

The entity reaches its satisfaction; it achieves its aim. What then? Here once more, and *in the fourth place*, God is at work. In this instance, God receives into his own existence whatever has been actualized, sifting out the good from the deviant or distorted. Then, *fifthly*, God harmonizes in his own life that which has been contributed to him. The reception and the harmonization are each part of the same readiness of the divine to accept, and to relate with whatever else has been contributed, what is done in the creation. The harmonization is made possible because in God's consequent aspect there is always a loving concern and care that 'nothing be lost which can be saved' and that all which can be 'saved' shall be used for the realization of the divine intention and the forwarding of the general over-all pattern which is basic in the cosmos as a whole.

Nor does the divine activity cease at this point. For in his superjective aspect God gives back to the creation, as a further responsive operation, the achievements which have been received, accepted, and harmonized in him. Purified through such harmonization, these are now open to divine employment for the furthering of love in the world. I have already quoted some words of Whitehead's which beautifully express this aspect of the divine activity:

> The perfected actuality . . . is transformed into a reality in heaven, and the reality in heaven passes back into the world. By reason of this reciprocal relation, the love in the world passes into the love in heaven, and floods back into the world (*Process and Reality*, p. 532).

Here Whitehead states in a vivid way what might otherwise have seemed a coldly abstract treatment of the matter. Precisely by thus speaking of 'the love in the world', 'the love in heaven', and the love that 'floods back into the world' we come to appreciate even more the appeal of the new model of God. Here is an account of the world which follows from our taking Love divine and cosmic as the best model for God, which redeems existence as we know it from the threat of triviality, meaninglessness, and frustration, and which provides exactly that feeling of cosmic 'refreshment and companionship' which working religion both requires and expresses.

When this model is adopted we can find an appropriate significance in much, if not all, that was said in the old model about the divine omnipotence, omniscience, omnipresence, infinitude, wisdom, righteousness, 'immensity', and the like. As these 'attributes of God' were presented in that old model, they inevitably suggested what indeed they were then intended to suggest: an absolutely impassible and self-sufficient deity who yet in some odd fashion was believed to care for, even to love, the creation. But with the use of the new model, they can have a highly relevant value in what I have styled an adverbial fashion. Let us look at them in this newer way.

Divine omnipotence need not mean sheer power nor the capacity 'to do anything'. Even in traditional theology the latter was never *really* intended, since in that theology God was said to be unable to 'do' what was illogical (such as squaring a circle), or contrary to his nature (such as evil – although here, unfortunately, by its talk about God's 'permissive will', it seemed to be contradicting itself). In the new model, however, omnipotence is an available word, although perhaps an unfortunate one, to get at the assertion that the one abiding, strong, indefatigable, and eventually triumphant power in the world is the divine Love in all its working. Hence it is not a matter of sheer coercion but rather of the ability of persuasion or Love to bring about a state of affairs in which it can reign triumphantly over all else. Yet it cannot do this by negating the freedom of the created occasions; for that would mean a contradiction of what persuasion or love is all about.

A friend of mine once said that he could accept what I have just written about the divine Love as the heart of deity, but if that Love is not to be defeated (my friend said) it must have resources of coercive power to enforce itself upon the world. I could only reply that in that case my friend did *not* accept the divine Love as the heart of reality and as the best model for deity. Love which is obliged to use coercion to secure the consent of those with whom it would work, is Love which has contradicted or denied itself. For it to use coercion would be to declare that in fact it is force and not Love which is at the heart of reality.

Certainly the appearances may *seem* to contradict the 'omnipotence' of Love. I should therefore prefer to translate the word found in the creeds, *pantocrator*, more accurately as 'sovereign rule' – and I have already discussed this point in the chapter dealing with evil in the world. But in the long run, which may indeed be a very long run, our new model insists that cosmic Love *is to be* victorious. That 'to be' is not irrelevant, in at least one sense, since God is not above and beyond succession. Yet he has all time, from everlasting to everlasting, in which to work out his intention. In any event, if at every moment he receives into his own life that which is achieved, harmonizes it in his own Love, and then lets it 'flood back' into the world, nothing 'saveable' is lost despite the appalling 'appearances' to which I have referred. There is tragedy here, because divine anguish knows and experiences creaturely anguish. But that anguish, as the first part of this chapter has urged, is of the very nature of genuine love, whether divine or human.

Then there is divine omniscience. With the new model, in which time is taken seriously, God does not have the sort of knowledge in which what at present is only possible is seen by him in its actualization. On the contrary, the cosmic Love has the true wisdom which is available to it. It knows what has happened, because it *has* taken place; it knows the various decisions which *might be made* at any given future moment; and it knows *as possible*, but not as if already made actual, what will be the consequences of this or that decision freely made by the created occasions. Thus there is no pre-ordination, no predestination, no determinism; but there is providence – a term from a Latin word which literally put into English means 'taking care of or seeing about'. Thus in each and every instance divine Love is active for the best good which by free decision any created agent may choose. A phrase in the Prayer of Thanksgiving in the Anglican communion service speaks of our doing 'such good works as thou hast prepared for us to walk in'. We *pray* that we may be empowered to do such good works as God would have us do; there is no coercion upon us so that we *must* do them, willynilly, nor is there any reason to assume that God forces them rather than (as indeed the prayer asserts) 'prepares' them for us as possibilities for our choice.

Or take divine omnipresence. This may now be interpreted as the availability of the divine Love to all people at all times and in all places and in any circumstance. With that wide availability there is also the divine readiness to cooperate in realizing and fulfilling the possibilities which are open to us. In the Epistle to the Romans, St Paul writes (in the correct translation of his Greek words), 'God works towards a good end, in all respects, for those who love him. . .' That text states the true meaning of omnipresence when this is coupled with omniscience.

We can look more briefly at some of the other 'attributes' of God which are found in traditional theology. Transcendence now can signify the inexhaustability of the cosmic Love; immanence, the unfailing presence of that Love in the whole creation. In the next chapter we shall add to these two a third, namely concomitance, to indicate that the divine Love is not only inexhaustibly more than, yet everywhere present within, the creation but is also alongside and with the creation at every point. The attribute of infinitude is another way of expressing both the mystery of the divine Love and its unlimited capacity to handle whatever happens anywhere. The divine wisdom is the profound knowledge of that Love, 'unto whom all hearts are open, all desires known, and from whom no secrets are hid'. Such Love knows 'what is in man', as the Fourth Gospel remarks about Jesus; it penetrates deep into the inside of existence at every level, and it always 'understands'. Righteousness is not abstract concern for justice, although it is indeed deeply concerned for such justice. Essentially it is the way in which cosmic Love seeks ever to bring about situations in which each will have what is due and each shall do that which it is his or her responsibility to do: to establish situations, circumstances, and a human society in which there is no servitude beyond that which human love takes upon itself and in which there is equality of opportunity for each person to realize, to the fullest possible extent, given human potentiality. And immensity is an old word which with the new model can signify once again that God is not confined to this or that particular place but is present, at work, and available always and everywhere.

It is perhaps unnecessary to continue along these lines. Anybody can go through the traditional listing of attributes and convert each of them into adverbs which tell us something about the loving activity in the world which is nothing other than the cosmic Lover who, in Dante's great phrase, 'moves the sun and the other stars' and who moves also in the lives of men and women, whoever and wherever they may be.

A Note on God and Other Worlds

We have just spoken of the way in which God who is cosmic Lover 'moves the sun and the other stars' and, as we added, moves also in the lives of men and women, whoever and wherever they may be. But what about the possibility of there being other inhabited planets in the universe – and other universes besides the one we know, with the likelihood that they too may include inhabited planets? In other words, what about God in relationship to what may well be a myriad of other worlds where conscious life exists?

One of the difficulties with the older and conventional models of God, which we have criticized for their inadequacy and even their grave misrepresentation of the Christian vision of God as 'pure unbounded Love', is that for the most part they have a thoroughly anthropocentric quality. Much of what they suggest depends upon a previous assumption that this world of ours and what happens to us human beings are the only really important things. They have often contributed to that exaggerated sense of our own human position which is part of the self-centredness that vitiates human existence.

Thus it is not surprising that when people who accept the picture of God as the guarantor of the *status quo*, the 'big man in the sky', and the like, are confronted with the high probability – or as some scientists now say, the absolute certainty – of untold millions of non-human intelligences in worlds remote from our own, they become alarmed and have a feeling that 'their' God is being taken away from them. They fear that the 'God of the universe', including in his concern all actual and possible kinds of worlds, will be the undoing of the God with whom, in Jesus Christ, Christians are so vitally concerned.

The real question here is not the astronomical intimidation felt by those who have learned of the enormous extent in space and duration in time of the created order. The real question is whether there can be any relationship between the divine reality we name God and have known in a decisive way in the event of Jesus Christ *and* the hypothetical inhabitants of other planets who obviously can know nothing of this historical event and its consequences. Whether those millions of created intelligences exist or do not exist is not a theological question; it is a problem for the scientists whose special interest is in astro-physics and associated disciplines. But there is a theological question, indeed a religiously important question, when we ask in what sense such creatures would be related to God.

Not only had the conventional picture of God a markedly anthropocentric quality. The event of Jesus Christ has also been interpreted in a too narrow perspective. But for anyone who is acquainted with the great tradition of Christian thought, not least in the days of 'the Fathers of the Church' during the first four or five centuries of the Christian era, there can be no doubt that the excessive 'Jesu-centrism' of post-Reformation theology has seriously misrepresented the situation. The classical christological position was never Jesu-centric in that narrow sense. Rather, Jesus was seen as the '*incarnation* of the Eternal Word of God'; and that specific human existence, lived in Palestine two thousand years ago, was not taken to be the whole story. In the event which classical theology called incarnation – that is, in the total reality we indicate when we say Jesus Christ – a clue was given to the true nature of God and a clue to the intended nature of humankind, hence also a clue to the relationship which obtained between God and the created order. In words which I have often used before, Jesus Christ as the focal enactment and expression of God in human terms was not thought to *confine* but to *define* God in his relationship to the creation.

Furthermore, the ancient creed commonly called Nicene, used regularly at the Eucharist in many Christian churches, speaks of what was done in Jesus Christ as 'consubstanial with', or of the 'same substance as' (using here, of course, the old substance philosophy which was dominant when the creed was composed), the divine reality (or 'Father') – that is with the basic divine grounding for the whole creation. To speak in that way is to assert that anything and everything that God does and is, no matter where and no matter whether on this planet or on some other, is 'all of a piece'. Thus Christian faith declares that *all* of God's activity is loving activity which is congruous with, although possibly very different in its specific mode of expression from, what has been 'determined, dared, and done' in Jesus of Nazareth. In all places and at all times, God's activity is activity in love, since God is everlasting Love. What is known in Jesus, declared vividly and with a quality of specificity so far as *we* are concerned, is identical with what God is doing everywhere else. God's eternal 'Word' is operative throughout the creation.

How God works with and for other created beings, if such do indeed exist, is quite beyond our human knowing. We have no information, certainly not at the present moment, about what is going on elsewhere. But we can be confident that if there is conscious life elsewhere, God has made available to such creatures some witness to what he is 'up to'. Years ago, C. S. Lewis had an essay in which he made just this point. But he was not alone in speaking along these lines. In Eric L. Mascall's *Christian Theology and Modern Science* (Longmans Green 1956) the same position was argued (pp. 36–45). Another theologian, Frank Weston, now largely forgotten but in his own day a thinker of great ability, wrote as follows:

> I do not know if other planets support rational life . . . If they do their religion will be the self-unveiling of eternal Love in terms and forms intelligible to them. Why may God not exhibit, on another planet, another activity of like kind? . . . It is only those who erect a false barrier between the universal activity of the Word and his incarnate life as man who will boggle at the possibility of his self-revelation in a created form on another planet (*The Revelation of Eternal Love*, Mowbrays 1920).

Again, the English Catholic poet Alice Meynell once wrote a remarkable poem called 'Christ in the Universe'. In that poem she spoke of 'the myriad forms' which God may have taken to disclose himself to those who live in the many different planets – ways which, to her mind, one day would be made known to us. On each of them, she said, God acts in an appropriate manner. For us human beings, however, there is the decisive event of Christ. That event gives us a key to *what it is all about*: and what it is all about is an enormous Love which by the necessity of its own nature must communicate itself to the creation. So *for us*, she wrote,

> With this ambiguous earth
> His dealings have been told us. These abide:
> The signal to a maid, the human birth,
> The lesson, and the young Man Crucified.
>
> (*Poems of Alice Meynell*, Scribners 1923, p. 92)

In an age when space-travel is with us, when the possibility and likelihood of other inhabited worlds is more and more a matter of discussion, such a position as Alice Meynell's and the others whom

I have just quoted may enable us to grasp how the new model of God is adequate, both by its stress on the divine Love and by its rejection of other pictures which are either too anthropocentric or too anthropomorphic, to our vastly expanded universe as well as to our inherited faith.

9

The Cosmic Lover as Source of Companionship and Refreshment

The phrase 'companionship and refreshment', which has already been used several times in this book, is taken from Whitehead, who used it to indicate what he believed the sense of the reality of God provides for men and women. In this chapter and under that heading I shall be considering what is commonly styled 'religious experience'. But I must warn the reader that I shall use the words in a much wider sense than is customary, for I wish to include in that experience more than the often-reported conscious awareness of a divine presence with, and a divine action upon, those who speak about it.

My reason for doing this has a certain history. My old teacher and friend, Professor Leonard Hodgson of Oxford, used to lament that in so much discussion of what it means to be religious, attention was focussed upon some specific and vivid awareness, some particular kind of religious consciousness, which is known to some people but by no means to everybody. He was prepared to suggest that physiological-psychological factors explained why some people have and others do not have this awareness or consciousness. But he insisted that we could more suitably think of the phrase 'religious experience' as pointing towards the totality of experience, had in many different areas and aspects of anybody's life when that person had faith in God and interpreted all that happened to him, and all that he was and did, as lived 'under God and for God'. Hodgson said that, much of the time, such an experience would be dim and inchoate, although there could indeed be occasions when it was much more vividly grasped as nothing other than a personal contact with the deity in whom the person had faith and to whom a commitment in faith had been made.

I am convinced that Hodgson was correct. Hence, while I shall indeed speak of religious experience in the narrower sense, I shall also say a great deal about aesthetic experience, the imperative to labour for justice and equity among human beings, and the deeply-known love which can be shared between or among men and women such as we are. It ought to be apparent that there are many other areas, too, which have or may come to have this 'religious' quality: for example, the scientist's dedication to the truth he hopes to discover; the devotion to duty found in people in various callings, such as medicine and nursing; the fulfilment of obligations in respect to family and friends whose welfare one wishes to promote. But I believe that the three areas I have chosen and just mentioned – aesthetic experience, the struggle for justice, and human love – will serve to indicate the main point that I am hoping to make: namely, that whenever and wherever human beings find dignity, purpose, significance, and value in their living, in those areas there is given refreshment, and not infrequently some awareness that one is 'going with the grain of the universe', cooperating with the basic thrust or drive through all things, and hence that one has a companionship which is more than merely creaturely, human, and finite.

But first it is necessary to direct attention to religious experience in the narrower sense.

There can be no question that very large numbers of men, women, and children, even in a highly secular age like our own, have just that kind of experience. They have a sense of a presence not themselves, which is with them in their moments of rejoicing and in their times of despondency. They speak about some more-than-human companionship which they know well. They tell us that in their times of prayer and worship they have become conscious that there is a 'Thou' in contact with their own 'I'. They speak about a strong feeling of forgiveness and acceptance which has come to them when they have acknowledged their inadequacy, their defection, their wrongs – which probably they would call by the ancient and familiar name of sin – receiving divine pardon and restoration. From the days when William James gave his famous Gifford lectures on *Varieties of Religious Experience*, there have been hundreds, indeed thousands, of careful studies of this subject from the psychological perspective and with due account taken of the kinds of background and environment characteristic of persons with such an experience. While some few experts have been prepared to dismiss the whole business as illusory – the classical instance is Sigmund Freud – the great majority

have concluded that however difficult it may be to account for and
explain what is going on, the plain fact is that large numbers of
entirely healthy, emotionally stable, and completely sane men and
women have testified to the reality of the experience; and they agree
that there is no reason to dismiss this testimony nor the reality to
which it bears witnesses, unless one illicitly intrudes philosophical
presuppositions which would inevitably make the experience seem
invalid.

It is not necessary to argue the case for the validity of this narrower
kind of religious experience; common sense requires us to accept it
for what it is. Such experience points to contact with some reality
greater than human which, in a fashion that is to us mysterious but
none the less genuine, makes its impact upon men and women of
most diverse cultures, races, classes, nations, and types. Usually there
is personal or private exercise in meditation or prayer which provides
the occasion for the experience, although it is also to be had in more
public ways, like services of worship in churches, synagogues,
temples, and shrines. In such moments, the divine is experienced in
personal relationship with men, women and children. Various models
for God may be in the minds of those who thus pray or meditate,
worship or adore. But the result of the exercise seems always to be
the companionship and refreshment to which Whitehead referred in
his discussion of religion. There is a feeling that contact is being had
with some 'grain of rightness' running through things, to use his
words; and, for vast numbers, this is not an impersonal grain but
somehow or other is possessed of the personal quality which makes
possible friendship or love with other persons. The religious experience is known in a fashion which is analogous to the kind of
relationship which we know between human beings.

The persisting witness to such experience is so strong that it cannot
be rejected. What is more, it is so strong that it can give us reasonable
assurance that in at least some respects there is what Coleridge once
called 'personeity' in the divine reality. It would be silly to think that
in God such a personal quality is identical with what we ourselves
know as personality. But nobody has ever really thought this to be
the case, once theological interpretation has been allowed. The simple
believer may talk as if he or she were describing a personal contact
such as would occur between John and Mary here and now in this
world. Yet even that simple believer knows that there is a difference;
the relationship is much more unpredictable in its occurrence, much
more mysterious in its working, and much more subtle in its consequences than the strictly human and mundane experience of personal
contact to which it is likened.

Let us grant, then, that there is for many precisely this narrower kind of relationship. But at the same time, let us concede that for many more such a contact is at most occasional and very sporadic, while for still others it is not known at all. These last men and women could never claim that they have had such moments. Yet this does not suggest, and for thoughtful inquirers should not imply, that such persons are without another sort of experience that has every right to be called 'religious' in Hodgson's broader interpretation.

For most people, the significant moments of life are those in which there is a deep awareness of love. I have already discussed what I called the phenomenology of love, human and divine. It will suffice to say here that when there is profound commitment to another, genuine mutuality or sharing of life, real concern for the realization of another's best possibilities, hopefulness or expectancy of that realization, and a human sense of fellowship or communion, we often are prepared to say, with some acquaintances of mine, 'This thing is bigger than either of us or than both of us together.' There is an intimation, experienced in genuine loving, of more than the merely human, important and central as that may be. So also, but obviously with less intensity, in our intimate friendships, and similarly in those moments with persons, who otherwise may be almost strangers, when we are aware of a 'more' which escapes precise definition but which brings us joy on some occasions and sadness on others. We are 'with' this or that other; yet we are also in the presence of that which seems to transcend the moment of delight or of sorrow.

If my view is correct about the way in which human sexuality in its broader sense is everywhere present, with its grounding in the physiology and psychology which is ours as human, we may very well say that human sexual experience is another intimation of that which is greater than ourselves. In moments of high sexual excitement, the partners will not have any vivid consciousness of this fact. It would be absurd if they attempted to analyse it in times of physical union or experienced it (as such) in anything like a vivid fashion. Yet there *is* that exaltation, that being lifted out of self into shared life with another, that feeling of fulfilment and self-realization with another of one's own kind, which bespeaks something much more profound than animal contact or rutting. There is a religious aspect in sexuality when it is more than sensuous gratification for its own sake; and conversely there is also a sexual aspect in religion, if by the word 'religion' we mean some recognition of the more-than-human in the world. Presumably this is why a good deal of religious talk has been in terms that have a sexual quality. It is why Roman Lull, for example, can write about religious devotion in a book called *The*

Book of the Lover and the Beloved; it is why we have in the Bible a Jewish love lyric, 'The Song of Songs'; and it is why it has not seemed improper for mystics to speak of the 'marriage of God and the soul' when the topic under discussion is loving contact between the divine and human.

In these days of women's liberation, we have writers who urge that the divine is 'above' sexual distinctions, male or female. I prefer to speak of the divine as *inclusive of all* that male and female denote and connote at the human level. God is our father *and* our mother; the pronouns 'she' and 'he' are equally appropriate if we purpose to talk of God in personal idiom rather than with neuter words like 'it'. Indeed, if what has been proposed earlier about the new model for God as the cosmic Lover tells us anything, it is *necessary* to have both feminine and masculine in the picture. The gracious, generous, receptive, responsive side needs emphasis just as much as faithfulness, prevenience of action, ordering, harmonizing, and luring. Thus I urge that we should have the courage to affirm the goodness of human sexuality and its intimations of the divine reality, once this has been redeemed from its tendency to slip back into the pre-human animal mating from which at some point in history it has so wonderfully emerged. Even more strongly, I urge that we need have no fear that thus to value sexuality will reduce piety to paganism and that the moral strain in all high religion will get lost in a sensuality without love, love's demands, and love's anguish.

I mentioned above another area of human endeavour which has religious implications: the concern for social justice, for the right of every human being, man or woman or child, to grow in dignity, to have personal integrity, and to be granted every opportunity to fulfil potentiality. For vast numbers of people today, this area is of supreme importance. Nor is it for them just a matter of fighting for the rights of others; it is not only a pragmatic interest. It is an imperative which is inescapable for these valiant people, who like the old American Quaker abolitionist John Woolman, have 'a concern laid on their hearts' to work for human equality, decency, respect, and dignity. But whence comes this concern which is felt so deeply in their hearts? Here, once more, I believe we may say 'there is something that is transcendent to the human'; there is a 'more' which speaks, however inadequately this may be recognized even by those who feel it so strongly, from a dimension in the world that is supra-human. The basic thrust or drive in things, the 'rightness' of which Whitehead spoke, is at work here.

But it is at work under an incognito, in disguise. This also is true in the aesthetic side of our human living, to which altogether too little attention has been given when an account is being made of what goes on in the depths of human existence.

Beauty, in the sense shortly to be defined, is a disclosure to us of the character of God himself, a revelation of something basic to and fundamental in the dynamic structure of the world. Beauty is no incidental or accidental matter. It speaks from the depths of the world and it speaks to the deep in human experience, bringing with it tidings of a level or dimension of reality which is much more important in its impact than the 'matter of fact' apperances which in so much of our life we take to be all there is. By speaking of beauty here I am not talking about the merely 'pretty', which may be attractive in a superficial manner but never gets 'through' to us in depth. The aesthetic (as the very Greek word *aisthesis* shows) has to do with what speaks to us so profoundly, with such an awakening of imaginative response, that we are changed after contemplating it.

Whitehead defined beauty as 'the mutual adaptation of the several factors in an occasion of experience' (*Adventures of Ideas*, p. 324). The objective reality meets with a subjective response, so that there is a feeling of satisfaction, yet without the surface emotionalism which is often mistaken for a sense of the aesthetically right or good. There is a 'splendour of form', in St Thomas Aquinas' words, in which there is a balancing of contrasts so that monotony or sheer 'sameness' is averted and violent conflict or an over-stressing of the contrasting elements is equally absent. Beauty has its objective side, in that *it is there* to be enjoyed; yet there must also be the subjective side, in that *there is a response* made from the percipient. Harmony appeals to feeling and feeling responds to harmony.

Without beauty, with its two sides, we humans are likely to experience the world around us in a literalistic and rationalistic fashion. Appreciation, evaluation, sensitivity, and wonder are absent from those who have not learned to respond aesthetically. The result has been an enormous impoverishment of our culture, since the confining of attention to that which is rationally or intellectually describable has meant that the evocative subtle nuances, both in experience and in the world, have been lost. We then become men and women whose existence has been so narrowed that we cannot grasp the glory, the mystery, the horror and delight, of that world and of our own human depths. We moralize ourselves and our experience, so that the 'good' gets interpreted almost exclusively as the 'right'; and we are unable to see that the genuine *bonum* or true 'good' has for its first meaning in human life that which, because of its intrinsic capacity to present and create harmony, is enticing and luring, awakening appetition or desire, and providing the sense of fulfilment which alone can bring us to true satisfaction. On the other hand, when there is an awareness of the 'beauty of goodness' and the 'goodness of beauty' (Plato's *kalagathon*), adjustment is made possible on our part to a basic harmony in things which is discovered *to us* much more than discovered *by us*. We can see the importance of Sir Herbert Read's demand that a considerable part of proper education is precisely in learning to appreciate – to delight in art of all sorts as more than just an expression of the human spirit, since we have been brought to understand that in such art there is indeed a disclosure to us of a *given* in the creation.

To speak in that way, however, is to say that created harmony is nothing other than a revelation of God as 'the altogether lovely'. This does not mean that beauty stands before us in some supposedly original 'completeness'. Like everything else in the world, it is part of a process which includes adventure and striving and an overcoming of the threat of disharmony. This is why the genuinely beautiful is always tragic. The beautiful is a conformation of elements or aspects of the creation in maximum mutuality or harmony so far as finitude will permit, where what emerges and is subjectively experienced is effective in bringing into creative tension what might well have been discordant and destructive elements. This requires the elimination of some possibilities; or their proper use, if they have a place, in contributing to a greater harmony. At the creaturely level this can never be fully achieved, to be sure; but there is a glimpse, even in such partial harmonization, of the perfected divine harmony and hence an opening to us of that divine joy which is God. In a world where all growth is with pain and where novelty calls in question superficial satisfaction, the beautiful is bound to be disturbing. To move from parochial contentment to a wider and more inclusive satisfaction makes us uncomfortable. Great poetry, music, dancing, portraiture, and sculpture do not make us 'feel nice'; rather, they bring about a certain unease. Yet at that very moment and in that very way, they awaken a desire for 'more'. And they convey a present sense of that 'more'.

What I have been saying should help us to distinguish between beauty and what earlier I called the merely pretty, which achieves its end by a rejection of contrasts or by a too ready appeal to the obvious. It should also help us to see that all great art requires striving. Not only is the composer, the painter, the sculptor, and the dramatist in anguish until delivered of this creative reality. The listener, the observer, and the audience for any art-form – be it poetry, sculpture, music, ballet, or theatre – is also made participant in an adventure which (as Whitehead urged) brings zest but also includes agony – and *agon* in the original Greek meant striving and struggle.

Yet through the agony, ecstasy is available; and with ecstasy there comes peace. This is not the peace which is the absence of all striving; it is the peace which is delight, attained through and in contrasts, whereby genuine harmony is found and enjoyed. We may properly say that this is one aspect of 'the peace of God which passes all understanding'. It is indeed God himself, felt as 'the harmony of harmonies' in whom the discordance known in creation has been reconciled in terms of '*valued* contrast'. Here is a joy that endures not passively but actively, as each small bit of created harmony provides the opportunity for further experiment, further experience, further delight. The beautiful in music, painting, poetry or dance is always evocative but never exhausted. It invites the beholder, listener, or participant to discover, often with pain, an ever deeper loveliness and thereby to experience ever fuller satisfaction. Beauty is a lure for us finite creatures, providing adventure and zest and promising harmony and peace.

I do not apologize for spending this much time and space on beauty and on the 'aesthetic component' (in Dr F. C. S. Northrop's words), since it is much neglected in religious discussion. It happens that I am a member of a college which has for its chapel one of the most beautiful examples of English Gothic architecture: King's College Chapel in Cambridge. We have a choir which is famous for its splendid rendition of music in worship and for its singing of other sacred song. Thousands of people come regularly to attend its daily services; others travel from the far corners of the earth to be present when the choir is singing Christmas music or the 'Advent Procession-al'. I am daily impressed by the way in which those who are present are caught up into the music. I see how often they are carried away by its sheer beauty. I think of T. S. Eliot's lines,

> Music heard so deeply that it is not heard at all,
> But *you* are the music, while the music lasts.

And afterwards, talking at the back of chapel to these visitors, I am confirmed in this impression. They may not know 'religious exper-ience' in the narrower sense; they may even have decided to come to our services only because it is the thing to do when one visits Cambridge. Yet I know from what they tell me that they have enjoyed what can only be called, and called with complete propriety, a 'religious experience'. They may not have had any vivid sense of companionship, but they have felt contact with a reality greater than themselves. Most certainly they have experienced a refreshment which sends them out of the chapel different people from what they were when they came in.

Granted that men and women can know a relationship with God through most various channels, such as the three I have mentioned, how may we best think of that God? I have proposed the new model of the cosmic Lover; but now I wish to go further and suggest that we may most adequately grasp the reality of that Lover if we see him as transcendent, in all his inexhaustibility and infinite resources; as immanent in the world, where he is active to awaken a response to his activity; and as concomitant with creaturely occasions as he lures and solicits their response. Obviously this three-foldness recalls the Christian doctrine of the triune God; and I believe that this is important to stress.

A conceptuality which uses the model of the divine reality as involved in, as constantly in relationship with, and as always active in the cosmos, can be ready to recognize distinctions in the modes of that involvement, relationship, and activity. I am not saying that there is necessarily a precise correspondence between the traditional doctrine and what is to follow, but I am prepared to argue that the doctrine is what Dr C. C. J. Webb once called it, 'an intimation', a hint or clue provided for us, of the diverse ways in which God is available for our responsive faith.

Let me put it in this fashion. God as cosmic Love is the worshipful and unsurpassable deity, *more than* the created order even if always active within it. The symbol for this is his 'fatherhood' – or 'motherhood', if one prefers, as I do, to employ the feminine as frequently as one does the masculine. God is the ultimate source of all novelty and the preserver of all order. God as cosmic Love is also *with* his creation, alongside it, providing it from 'alongside' with lures and invitations to continue the creative advance in the direction of fuller and more adequate actualizations of love, such as can give existence its true worth or importance. The symbol for this is the *Logos*, 'the Self-Expressive Word' or concomitant activity of God, whose luring and soliciting finds for Christian faith a decisive and focal human enactment in the man Jesus. And finally God as cosmic Love is *within* the creation, to enable from it a response to lure and invitation which will bring the created occasions to contribute (by their own freely-chosen decisions) to the intention of God, an intention which is nothing other than realization of their potentiality and hence can become their creaturely contribution to the enrichment of deity himself. The symbol for this is the Spirit, operative not only in human experience and human history but in the natural order as well.

I find here suggestive, if not exact, associations with the aspects of

God as primordial, consequent, and superjective, to which I have referred in earlier chapters. I also find a welcome emphasis on the cosmic and secular areas as included within the divine activity. The classical triunitarian symbol cannot be pressed to fit precisely into this Process pattern. But it can remain an invaluable symbol which is helpful in worship, which links present-day Christians with their ancestors in the faith, and which opens up speculative and practical experiential possibilities that may be richly rewarding as we attempt to explore more and more fully what we mean when we speak about God and attempt to live in conscious and intentional relationship with him.

Here is no odd bit of theological mathematics. Of course there have been theologians who have treated it as such, with their puzzlement about how 'one' can be 'three' and 'three' can be 'one'. Such theologians seem to me to have missed the point, quite as much as those others who have simply rejected out-of-hand what triunitarian talk suggests. Let us respect the symbol but not press it to absurd lengths; let us allow it to illuminate our thinking about deity; and let us value above all the way in which, when appropriately used and seriously understood, it enables us to speak of the mystery of Godhead as Love. It is not an incredible statement of contradictions but a safeguard for all that is best, most enriching, most vitalizing, most satisfying (even if also most disturbing) in our 'religious experience'.

10

Some Implications: Theological, Liturgical, Moral

The model for God as the cosmic Lover commends itself to us because it is religiously relevant, philosophically intelligible, and scientifically acceptable. It tells us that God is to be seen as primarily Love-in-Act, who 'is what he does'; who is at work in the creation; who is 'time-full' since history matters for him and in him; who respects and values creaturely freedom and the responsibility which attaches to decisions made in that freedom; who is disclosed through his activity in nature and history but for Christian faith decisively and definitively in the man Jesus; who receives into his own life what is accomplished for good in the world; who can transmute the actual evils in that world into occasions for further good; and who is enduringly faithful and can be trusted to support all who cooperate with him in the creation of opportunities for abundant life in love and goodness and with concern for righteousness and equity.

If we are prepared to accept this new model, we have a criterion for all our further theological understanding. Insofar as any phase in such theological development is in accordance with or implied by the criterion of Love-in-Act, we can find value in it. Insofar as any phase is irreconcilable with that criterion or minimizes or modifies it so that it no longer means what it says, that development is to be rejected and can have no place in responsible Christian interpretation of God, the world, or human existence.

Now it is obvious that in the face of that criterion, a good deal that we find in our conventional theology is in need of radical revision. Likewise, it is obvious that much in Christian liturgy or forms of worship, as well as in our common teaching about personal prayer and devotion, is equally in need of radical revision. Finally, it is obvious that much moral teaching must be radically changed if it is to meet the criterion of God as Love-in-Act and thus to guide the right growth of men and women so that they will reflect such Love and be open to serve as its instrumental agency.

I shall make suggestions in this chapter about some of these necessary revisions, all of them implicit in the use of the new model for God. What will emerge, once we have taken this task seriously and engaged in it patiently, will be a theology, a liturgy, and a moral imperative that will be more intelligible but also more biblical. I have pointed out that there is a remarkable congruity between the basic affirmations of biblical faith and this new model, when we have emancipated ourselves from the outworn and incredible literalism which has so tragically been associated in many minds with the claim to loyalty to scripture. In fact, that literalism, with its assumption of the inerrancy of each and every section of the Bible, is a denial of the whole movement of experience and thought of which the scriptures themselves are a record from the days of primitive Yahwism to full flowering in the life of Jesus and the early Christian witness to him. I have just said literalism; but that is not quite the proper word, since biblical fundamentalism sometimes resorts to a quite extraordinary twisting of the literal sense of some passages of scripture in the attempt to preserve the supposedly utter inerrancy of the material. The point is clear enough, however. If we are to see the Bible in the proper light, we shall recognize that it is the story of an ever more profound insight into the divine reality, as great Jewish seers and sages meditated on their own experience, on the history of their people, and on the impact which in their belief God was making upon them. The Bible is not a religious, theological, or moral dictionary or encyclopedia, but an astounding literary witness to living experience and to the realities which made that experience a genuine reality in the lives of those who have given us the material.

I begin our discussion with what is close to each of us and inescapable for our existence as men and women: what it means to be human. Nor is this the wrong place to begin, for we have already said something about the consequences of the change in approach of our thought about the attributes of God when the new model is accepted. We have urged that human existence can be indicative of the fashion in which we are to envisage everything else in the world. This is because human life and natural existence are so intimately related. We have emerged from the world of nature; and the right interpretation of our humanity will be an important clue to the natural order from which we have emerged and of which we are still a real although distinctive part. Conversely, what we say about God will be reflected in how we understand ourselves.

In earlier discussion I have spoken of human existence as a 'becoming' and a 'belonging'. I have also noted the fact that with the emergence of the specifically human much has been changed; for example, sexuality has become essentially unitive rather than merely reproductive. Bearing all this in mind, we may proceed to some further description of human existence in the light of the new model for God.

Since each entity is a particular focus of cosmic energy, an event, we must see that when we speak of the human we are not talking about some finished and completed substance which could be called human nature. Rather, we are talking about a movement or direction in which potentialities, themselves 'given' when this or that occasion appeared, are on the way to being actualized or made real and hence are moving towards a state of 'satisfaction'. Each of us is a series of moments of experience, linked together and given identity; by the reality of the past which is inherited and provides the raw material for development; by the way in which decisions are taken from moment to moment towards an aim or goal which was initially given but is now to be accepted by each for himself or herself; and a moving towards a future in which that goal will be achieved or in which through those decisions the goal will be rejected. Thus we can see that among other characteristics of human existence there will be a dependence upon the natural order, upon others of our kind, and upon the thrust or drive we call God, whether this last is recognized and acknowledged as such or is not recognized and consciously accepted. Again, there will be a dynamic activity in which significant choices are being made. There will be a capacity for relationships of varying intensity, which include the sharing of life with others in love, friendship, neighbourliness, and the like. There will be the relative freedom, inevitably within limits, to which we have given so much attention in these pages.

Human 'beings' – a word which is inaccurate, since in fact we are a 'becoming', but which we may use for convenience' sake to denote the particularity attaching to each of us – are not all exactly identical. There is a speciality for each, since each has its own past, its own kinds of decision among relevant possibilities to be actualized, and its own goal or end. Thus, there is a distinctiveness about every human existence, within the broader generality of that existence.

Again, we are more or less rational, more or less sensitive, more or less aware of ourselves as we become aware of others. Our human existence is a complex physical-mental-emotional affair, in which our body is as much ourselves as our capacity to think or will. I have often quoted in other books the comment of Gabriel Marcel that we do not 'have bodies' but 'are bodies'. It is equally correct to say that we do not 'have minds' but 'are minds' and that we do not 'have wills' but 'are wills'. In other words, we are a unity of what can be called the material and the spiritual. The purpose of our existence in its broadest sense is to realize more and more adequately this unity of selfhood. By memory, anticipation and hope we realize our own identity, so that each of us knows what it is to say 'I'. Even in the most intimate union of body, mind and emotions in the acts of loving, we are still each one himself or herself – this is why there is *union* and not a merging into some amorphous 'humanity', as if we were to lose ourselves in a literal sense. On the contrary, the meaning of 'loss of self' is essentially a rediscovery of basic selfhood in our association with those for whom we care.

With so much said, we can now proceed to the Christian affirmation that, at the human level, the goal or purpose of the whole movement is towards our becoming more genuinely human. With the recognition of the new model of God, this will tell us that we are by intention becoming *lovers*, created and finite and also defective (about this last we shall speak in a moment) – we are lovers-in-the-making. The Christian perspective, with its grounding in God as cosmic Lover, tells us that to become such created lovers, as we are meant to become, is a matter of our reflecting the cosmic Love itself as we move more and more towards the sharing of life. This might well be called a movement 'towards the image of God' who is Love and who for Christian faith has 'imaged' his Love definitively in the man Jesus. But there is also an opening of self to the vocation of serving as a personalized instrumental agency for the divine Lover. This is not by any imposition upon us or by any force exercised upon us in such a way that our free assent is denied. The way in which love, whether divine or human, does its work is through lure towards responsive love; and therefore by our own decisions, made with due awareness of our accountability, we can act as surrogates of the divine Love in our doings, actions, and thoughts. Note that I have said surrogate, not substitute. In all our human integrity we *exist*; God respects and values that existence. We cannot substitute anything else, since in truth there is nothing else which we might become. On the other hand, we can consciously decide to act as surrogates or agents for the divine Love, moving as it does in the world for the most part through creaturely agencies. In thus deciding, and in consequence thus being ready to act, we become *ourselves*: or in the words of another theologian, 'We are enabled to become what by the divine purpose we always are.'

One of the implications of the new model for God, therefore, will be a different way of understanding human existence. Our 'doctrine of manhood' (and womanhood, too, of course) will reflect what is believed about God. The tragedy of human existence is that our choices most of the time, if not always, are in a direction which impedes or rejects just such a possibility of created loverhood. And this brings us to the question of human sin.

In many traditional theologies, sin has been defined in terms of the violation of laws or commandments given by God and imposed upon his children. Such a view is not biblical, since the Bible sees human sin as primarily a breaking of intentional relationships between God and humanity or among men and women. Our basic sin is our refusal to grow in a relationship with God, which will be reflected in our human relationships. Hateful, cruel, selfish, or careless attitudes and actions towards other humans will be nothing other than implicit breakings of our relationship with God who is Love.

Here we must remember also the circumstances which the long human history of such wrong decisions has brought about, so that 'we cannot do what we would' and 'we do what we would not' in our participation, by our inescapable social belonging, in the human condition as it is sadly alienated from the divine Lover and thus estranged from its genuine possibilities. The Christian 'good news' is that there is a 'way out' for men and women. God has acted and he continues to act to establish what may be variously styled 'redemption', 'salvation', or 'newness of life' for his children. Thus we come to the significance of 'atonement', as theologians would put it.

The model of God as cosmic Lover, combined with awareness of basic biblical insights, delivers us from barbarous and immoral doctrines of atonement which have talked about God's 'buying back' his children from control or possession by the devil. It rules out once and for all any teaching which portrays God as requiring some sort of price to be paid for the satisfaction of his justice – a price which his incarnate Son is supposed to have paid. The kinds of atonement doctrine which speak in such terms are impossible when we have made central to our faith God as 'pure unbounded Love'. A reconstruction of doctrine here will take very seriously 'at-one-ment' as the meaning of the traditional word: a bringing into unity of the divine Lover and the defective, erring, tragically unloving human, by an act in which that divine Lover takes the first steps in loving and thereby wins a response of returning love from his children. Abelard saw the main point here, but his teaching has been greatly misunderstood. Yet it is also true that the Aberlardian insight requires an ontological grounding, such as is provided by the Process insistence on love as no merely human affair, but as the basic dynamic of the cosmos. This profound Love, which is at the heart of things, *acts* in the world; and it acts nowhere so decisively as when it makes available to men and women, with their deep awareness of failure and of their wilful rejection of love human as well as Love divine, the renewed and renewing possibility of life-in-Love itself.

In Jesus Christ, says Christian faith, God re-presented this seeking love which is his own nature and character. In what Jesus did and was, there was an expression (defined as decisive for us humans but not confined only to the event of Christ) of the divine concern for human existence at all times and places. To respond to that, once it has been vividly presented, and to let it work itself out in one's own life, *is* to be redeemed or saved.

How is this done? By God's acting towards us, in our concrete situation of alienation and estrangement, as if we were already 'in Christ'. This is the goal of human existence because to be 'in Christ' is nothing other than to be 'in Love' – for Jesus Christ is the expression of divine Love and is in himself a genuine human loving which acts for and enacts the divine Love. Traditionally this has been stated by talk about the intimate association of the doctrines of incarnation and atonement. But it is not necessary to use either word to state what is taking place.

As we have observed, the word 'atonement' can serve well if it is broken down as I have suggested. The word 'incarnation', however, can lead to, and often has led to, much misunderstanding. It has been taken to mean that in Jesus there is the one and only instance of divine creative and redemptive activity in the world; or it has seemed to set up some *tertium quid*, the 'God-Man', who is regarded as anomalous and entirely unparalleled. Recent writers have correctly pointed out that incarnation is a valuable but inescapably mythological term to express the abiding Christian conviction that 'in Christ God was reconciling the world to himself'; and that in this event faith has been enabled to see the divine activity of Love moving through and acted out in a human activity of loving. This point could lead us into a lengthy discussion of christological questions; but I shall content myself with a brief treatment which I hope may be suggestive.

Christian faith has consistently maintained that in some genuine fashion there is in Jesus Christ an interaction of God and human life, however varied may have been the ways in which this conviction has been expressed. Chalcedon (AD 451) affirmed such a 'union' in its own idiom, stressing that true God and true man are in that historical event related in a manner which was defined by four adverbs: 'unchangeably, unconfusedly, indivisibly, and inseparably'. But the idiom of the theologians at Chalcedon is not ours. They thought in terms of 'natures' and 'substances' and the like; we think in terms of event, activity, becoming, and belonging. Our task is to affirm the basic Christian conviction; but in doing so we must employ language available to us in our own time. Process Thought provides such a language.

We have seen that for the Process conceptuality the world is dynamic and marked by 'becoming'; its constituents are events which are interactive and inter-related; its creaturely decisions 'matter and have consequences', in Whitehead's words; and love (or 'persuasion') receives an ontological status so that it is taken to be the ultimate reality, supreme, dependable, worshipful, and unsurpassable.

The biblical story is the tale of God's disclosing himself in act to his human children, as they were able to receive and grasp what took place and to interpret it in relation to the rest of their experience. First conceived as sheer power, God was later seen as more than that: God was 'power that makes for righteousness', then as loving care (or *chesed*), and finally, in the New Testament witness, as seeking for response and luring the human race to live in *shalom* or abundant life, made available through an act of signal importance in the historical reality of Jesus, by his life, action, teaching, death, and victory. What God there *did* was what God *was*. Whitehead's aphorism, quoted several times in this book, 'a thing is what it does', finds special illustration in the event of Jesus Christ and what that event brought about in the affairs of humanity. And here there was divine prevenience *and* human response, focusing as in a point the God-human relationship; this was no supreme anomaly but the classical instance of what God is always up to and hence what God is always doing.

Now in Process Thought, the relationship between God and the world is such that God influences and affects the world, while the world also influences and affects God. However God is not identical with the world; he is transcendent over it while also immanent and active within it. Furthermore, certain events in that world are more significant or important than other events, because they more adequately sum up the past, make their impact in the present, and open up richer possibilities for the future. Christian faith sees in Jesus Christ just such an event, not absolutely unique and therefore unknowable but with a specificity and speciality which demand interpretation.

If this be the case, how can we speak meaningfully of one in whom God and human existence are 'unchangeably, unconfusedly, indivisibly, and inseparably' at one? The Process insight that Love is the basic motif in the cosmos assists us at this point. If we take that Love with utmost seriousness, we can glimpse how there can be a uniting of divine creative and receptive activity and human responsive activity. Above all, if Love is God's 'root-attribute', so that it defines deity for us, we have an invaluable clue to what talk of incarnation (whether we like that word or would prefer some other) is getting at. I shall develop this in a moment.

For the present, let me remark that the use of wrong models has been christologically disastrous. If we talk about two independent 'substances', God and manhood, we have difficulty in bringing them together without giving one or the other priority in which Jesus becomes God disguised to look like a man *or* a man supremely inspired by God, and not one in whom there is a genuine uniting, with each remaining itself but in union with the other. If we talk of two wills, conceived (as has usually been the case) in a coercive fashion, the only possible union would reduce Jesus to a man obedient to God's will *or* to a human will lost in the divine will. If we talk about two consciousnesses, there could only be a human consciousness illuminated by God *or* a divine replacement of the human consciousness by the divine 'mind'.

On the other hand, if we are bold enough to take Love as our basic model, a genuine union is possible without reduction or negation of either the divine or the human. If human life is being created to move on towards 'becoming a lover', to respond to the lure of initiating, prevenient, and outgoing divine Love and to contribute this response to God the final recipient, we have a meaningful approach to interpreting the speciality of God's action in the manhood of Jesus. The human analogy of love, lovers, and loving can then be used, always guarding against the obvious defections, limitations, and deficiencies known in our human experience. Of course any analogy is inadequate to God and God's ways in the created order; but this one seems our most valuable and useful one. It is a tragedy that theologians have often failed to employ it in christology because of these possible dangers. But I shall now use that analogy as our best and dominically validated insight into God's relationship with his children, supremely for our present purpose in the instance of Jesus Christ, his son, our brother, and our Lord.

First, there is prevenience. Someone moves towards us in love. That love provides an initial aim for our lives. We are awakened to respond to it. To know oneself loved is to be given a purpose towards the realization of which, as our own subjective aim, we thereafter give ourselves. We are invited to give more of ourselves to the one who first has loved us; we are enabled to do what otherwise would be incredible or impossible; we discover depths in ourselves which we did not know were there, precisely because the love wherewith we are loved reveals them and then strengthens us towards them. More and more, as the loving relationship grows and deepens, we live in our lover and our lover lives in us; we two find ourselves 'becoming one', yet without in any way damaging or reducing the integrity of our respective personhoods. Far from that; because each of the lovers becomes a more *real* person in this increasingly intimate relationship. The lover 'receives' the beloved and is enriched by this relationship. Thus to love is truly to live: as the recusant English poet Robert Southwell said, 'Not where I breathe but where I love, I live.' All of us, body and mind and spirit, is included in that mode of union; for I love with my whole self or I do not really love at all.

If we apply this analogy to the union of God and human existence in Jesus Christ, we can see at once its relevance. God is prevenient to this humanity; God gives the initial aim or vocation, which is to bring others to God through a life open to God at every point. God takes into himself that which the human life achieves. The divine activity is continually present; the human response is likewise continually present. Both are operative, but each is itself. Here we do not have two independent 'substances' or two striving wills or two differing consciousnesses, but a personal and personalizing relationship affecting both sides, with gracious giving and gracious receptivity. There is nothing static or mechanical about it. It is not strange that Theodore of Mopsuestia spoke of marriage as the best analogy here and used the words *eudokia* (God's delight in the beloved) and *synapheia* (personalizing union) to describe how God could be in Jesus 'as in a son' who was the 'well-beloved one'. Theodore's difficulty was that in his middle Platonic philosophical orientation God was too transcendent to make the union with humankind complete and full, try as hard as Theodore did. His christological insight, however, seems to me exactly right. It is in line with the Hebrew stress on activity and dynamism, with a genuine safeguarding of the manhood of the Lord through whom God has been disclosed as actively at work and whose total existence has now been 'taken into', or received by, God as an enduring reality in the divine life.

The union of these two, Godhead and humanity, in the deep mutuality of love makes possible a 'two-ness in one-ness'. 'I am in the Father and the Father in me', the Fourth Evangelist has Jesus say; hence he can also have him say, 'I and the Father are one'. The mutual indwelling of divine prevenient Lover and human responsive lover established a unity which was full and rich, complete and effective, with consequences both for God and human existence. There could be no more adequate union between God and man than such an one, in human love and in divine Love. Furthermore and finally, the total event is received into or taken up to be part of God in his consequent nature – God as affected by the creation – and therefore is now and forever integral to the divine life and to the working of God in the world. This, I take it, is what the resurrection 'myth' is telling us.

That all this in fact occurred in Jesus Christ cannot be demonstrated. We do not have the historical material that would compel us to say this. The New Testament is a witness to events which make possible such an affirmation; but there is no way in which the gospels can be forced to demonstrate its reality. This is a deliverance of faith. Yet it is not a blind faith nor a 'leap in the dark'. It makes sense of what material we *do* have; above all, it is confirmed in experience by those who live in terms of this affirmation: *solvitur ambulando*. The New Testament is written 'from faith to faith'; and in all faith there is inevitably a risk which the Christian tradition in which we stand and by which we live has been prepared to take. This requirement for risk, with the decision it demands, is inevitable since even if Love is indeed supreme it does not and cannot coerce belief. It can only invite it, asking for a free decision from those to whom it is presented as a viable, life-giving, and rewarding possibility.

There are many other important theological issues which might be mentioned here but there is not space to develop them. I can only hope that what has been said so far about human existence, human wrong, human redemption and the person of Christ will serve as an indication of the approach which will be necessary if we take seriously the new model of God. I move on now to say something about worship and prayer, as they too can undergo revision in the light of that model.

There can be little doubt that the language used in public worship, as well as in the canticles and hymns sung in divine service, will have a great deal to do with the way in which God, human response, and the entire Christian enterprise are understood by ordinary men and women. There is also little doubt that the liturgical idiom and the hymnody commonly found in worship is usually a reflection of the old model of God. It would be instructive to go through the traditional books of common prayer of the various churches of the Anglican communion, or the usual service books of most Lutheran bodies, or the older Roman Catholic form for the celebration of mass, and cite phrase after phrase which not only suggests but seems to declare clearly and unmistakeably that God is to be pictured as a tyrannical ruler seated on his celestial throne and surrounded by a court of heavenly creatures. The position of his worshippers in his presence is portrayed as cringing submission before a despotic figure. Indeed the whole thing all too often bears no relationship whatsoever to a loving relationship in which the cosmic Lover is adored by those whom he wishes to grow in stature, to reflect the Love which is his own innermost nature, and to share with him in a common enterprise of co-creation and fellow-working.

The Roman Catholic church undertook a radical revision of the mass, thanks to the Second Vatican Council. As mass is at present celebrated, it resembles much more a loving family meal, in which all present participate and in which God is worshipped as the heavenly parent who seeks only the best good of his children. The old language of the sultan's court has gone completely. The change was a great shock for many who had become so accustomed to the more traditional mode that they felt deprivation and sometimes reacted violently about what had been 'done to them'. For one thing, they claimed, the old sense of mystery was no longer felt in the mass; the service seemed altogether too familiar and human.

One can appreciate this reaction, but one need not agree with it. It is always hard for people who have been brought up for the whole of their lives to engage in one kind of liturgical action to make the tremendous readjustment which the newer forms require. Yet they were wrong in saying that mystery in the presence of the Holy God had been abolished. On the contrary, what has happened is the relocation of the mystery, finding it much more in the relationship between the divine Lover and the children of his Love than in that between a monarch and his subjects. Slowly, but surely, ordinary Roman Catholic laypeople are coming to see this. Holiness is now seen to mean the real distinction between the totally loving one who is to be adored and the sadly loveless ones who come into his presence in the liturgical action. Or as a contemporary French writer has put it:

> The revelation of this unique God . . . so ready to give himself, calls forth adoration and thanksgiving in the hearts of believers. Adoration means wondering but fearless silence, in which words are cut short, rendered powerless by joy at the Patience, the Loving-kindness, the radiant Goodness which has been poured forth throughout the course of history. The world is indeed shot through with Beauty, like a face suffused with happiness. Man pauses and discovers it is good to be alive. Thanksgiving is my

acceptance of this Love, in the certainty that my real place is in this sun, my heart open like an extended hand. Thirst has brought me to the source and my heart has become a fountain.

This quotation is from Paul Guèrin's *I Believe*, an English translation of which appeared in 1977 from Mayhew-McCrimmon in Britain. Guèrin's book is full of gems like the one just quoted, although sadly enough it still has a few traces of the old model of God, despite his best effort to stress always the centrality of love in the liturgical and theological enterprise of the Roman Catholic church.

In a similar fashion, Anglican and Lutheran revision has been concerned to alter the more outrageous monarchical language. The difficulty with much Anglican and Lutheran revision is that it has not been sufficiently based upon the newer theological understanding. It has been much more an attempt to return to ancient liturgical practice, on the one hand, and to modernize the language used in worship, on the other. Further, our newer ways of seeing the Bible and interpreting the biblical development in understanding God's nature and God's activity have not been taken seriously enough; hence newer liturgies often seem to treat scripture, and use biblical material, in a literalistic fashion, as if its mere quotation lent validity to some bit of liturgical action or affirmation. The result is a strange hodge-podge of good and bad. For example, in most revisions by the various branches of the Anglican communion admirable changes are made in the eucharistic Prayer of Consecration, so that Jesus' death is no longer the single point of departure but rather is seen in the context of his total life and mission. Yet at such a crucial point as the *Sanctus* ('Holy, Holy, Holy'), the revisions are prepared to accept, as does the Roman Catholic church, the new agreed translation in which there is not a word about the divine Love but rather stress on God's 'power and might' – which when put into modern English is even more difficult than the ancient and pictorial Jewish language about the 'Lord God of hosts' from which the *Sanctus* is derived.

What is needed, I urge, is a much more radical revision all the way through. Historical considerations are indeed important, since contemporary Christian worshippers are members of a community which they did not create nor establish, but into which they have been incorporated by baptism, and in which they now stand. But when the new insight centred in the divine Love is given its rightful priority, historical continuity can be preserved in some other fashion than by retaining or even (as sometimes happens) intensifying, because of the vernacular idiom, ideas that are not religiously valid and that are often theologically erroneous.

In the non-liturgical churches, a remarkable growth of interest in more formal services of worship, and away from the older very free ways, is to be observed. The excessive didacticism, which from the Reformation onward seems to have been characteristic of churches in the Calvinist and Zwinglian traditions, has been removed. But here again, the sad fact is that in a welcome return to more ordered worship, the tendency in many service books of these non-liturgical churches has been simply to copy, with slight modification, the older formulae of the Roman Catholic, Anglican and Lutheran churches.

Thus we may say that with the exception of many of the Roman Catholic alterations, there has not been anything like sufficient recognition of the need for very serious alteration in the language of worship. However, there is one area in which this kind of necessary change appears to have been understood. This is in the teaching about personal prayer, through the preparation and publication of many new manuals or guidebooks to that aspect of Christian devotion. The same is true of the hymns which have recently been written. As poetry they may be less attractive than the older and more traditional hymnody, but they have grasped the centrality of Love and their stress is much more familial than courtly.

In the matter of personal prayer, we are now being told frankly that this is not to be regarded as what Dean Inge once called 'a pestering of deity' by our petitions. We are no longer allowed to think that somehow if we act submissively we can force God to give us what we suppose we need or want. The teaching found in the classical masters of prayer has again come to the fore. Prayer is the 'attentive presence of God', the turning of our whole being to him so that we are made aware of the one who is always there. It is 'the elevation of the human personality to God', with the urgent desire to enter into a real communion with him. It is what the French Père Jean de Caussade urged centuries ago; the 'abandonment' of our human existence to the reality of God in the 'present moment', where his lure and invitation can be known and where his human children can be opened to respond to that solicitation. Perhaps what is most needed in this area of religious life is a more carefully thought out and more adequately presented account of the *working* of prayer, interpreted theologically. I believe that this will be forthcoming, since the newer teaching about *how to pray* will inevitably lead to a greater concern about *what* prayer accomplishes and how it does this.

I have mentioned the newer hymnody, which it seems to me is one of the places where we find most ready recognition and use of the imagery of love and justice and where the model of the divine Lover is most plainly seen. I shall give here one example of what I have in mind. This is a contemporary Roman Catholic hymn which is probably not an outstanding piece of poetry but most certainly communicates the sense of the divine Love:

> Where charity and love prevail
>   There God is ever found;
> Brought here together by God's love
>   By love are we thus bound.
>
> With grateful joy and holy fear
>   His charity we learn;
> Let us with heart and mind and soul
>   Now love him in return.
>
> Forgive we now each other's faults
>   As we our faults confess;
> And let us love each other well
>   In Christian holiness.
>
> Let strife among us be unknown
>   Let all contention cease;
> Be his the glory that we seek,
>   Be ours his holy peace.
>
> Let us recall that in our midst
>   Dwells God's begotten Son;
> As members of his Body joined
>   We are in him made one.
>
> No race nor creed can love exclude
>   If honoured be God's name;
> Our brotherhood embraces all
>   Whose Father is the same.
>
> (By Omer Westendorf; included
> in *The Monthly Mass Book*, USA)

I make no apology for quoting this hymn in full, because it provides a useful transition to the final topic in this chapter: the modification of moral ideas which is required by the adoption of the new model for God. The hymn speaks of the love by which we are bound, which we are to share, and which will lead us to seek the best for our brothers and sisters of any race or creed; and it suggests that the one moral absolute taken to be binding is God himself conceived as the self-giving divine Lover who wants from his human children their cooperation in his 'amorizing' project in the world.

To a great many people, within and without the Christian churches, the moral teaching of the Christian tradition has been primarily a matter of obedience to rules, codes, laws, and commandments. These have been exalted to a position of such supreme importance that it has been forgotten that they are, all of them, products of an age in which God was looked upon as essentially a moral governor – even a moral tyrant – who was to be obeyed without question. Certainly the new model understands God as morally concerned; but the notion of his 'governing', in the sense of imposing laws upon his children, no longer has much meaning. Rather, we are in the position where we can much more usefully engage in a radical revision of the mediaeval conception of the 'natural law'. This had its basis in a recognition of God as in his own nature and character identified with what was then called 'the eternal law'. That 'eternal law' was God's nature as moral; and it was reflected in the created world which when it was 'working' in the proper fashion was itself a moral order, so that to 'live in accordance with nature' *meant* to live 'in accordance with God's purpose'. to think, speak, or act *unnaturally*, in a manner less than, or otherwise than human, was to be 'in sin', because it was contrary to God's nature.

In another book, *Loving Says It All* (Pilgrim Press 1978), I have argued the case for such an approach as I now propose. The older formulation is not entirely satisfactory, above all in its constant talk of 'law'. But suppose we say that God is utterly and absolutely loving; that *this* is his nature and character. We can then go on to say that in the created order, which in its very creation is 'good' (as Genesis tells us, reflecting a deep Hebrew insight), there is given enough awareness (however vague or dim) of that divine Love to make us see that when and as and if humans are striving to live in genuine human love – not in sentimentality nor emotionalism, but in unswerving concern for the best good of others, with the search for justice and equality for all God's children – they are then living in accordance with the divine intention.

We fail over and over again. The inherited accumulation of wrongdoing throughout human history makes such living very difficult but not entirely impossible. And in any event, men and women are victims of their own selfish and self-centred preferences and prejudices. All this is true enough. Yet the moral imperative is to live in such love; and the grounding for that imperative, and the power or grace to move towards such loving, is the divine Love itself. Thus, 'where charity and love prevail, there *God* is ever found'. Or in the magnificent words from the old Roman Catholic liturgy for Holy Week: *ubi caritas et amor ibi Deus*: 'Where loving concern and caring are seen, there God is'. To 'obey God', then, is to seek to live in such loving concern and caring. That is the true meaning of

Christian morality; and its corollaries in our day-to-day existence are challenging to our easy and superficial acceptance of 'whatever goes'. Morality is then vital, demanding, stern; but it is also enriching and enabling.

11

God and the World's Destiny

Love is central in the model for God which we are presenting and defending: God is the cosmic Lover. He is creative in the world, for which he supplies both the ordering and the possibility of realizing novelty. He is responsive to the world, since he adapts and adjusts himself to the circumstances and situations in which that world is to be found at every moment, through the decision of its constituents made in the relative freedom that belongs to them and in the causative power which is proper to them. He is receptive of the world, because he accepts into his own life, for harmonization and for employment in further activity towards that world, that which is achieved by the created occasions. All the way through, and in every respect, he is intimately related to the world with which he identifies himself in loving care and in gracious readiness to assist, so that each and every world-event, if it so chooses and so acts, may realize the potentiality which is proper to it. What then is the world's destiny, in and with and under such a cosmic Lover? That is the subject of this chapter. Our discussion here must be brief but my position has been developed at some length in my *After Death - Life in God* (SCM Press 1980).

In much traditional theology, the created order is regarded as unimportant to the divine reality. It is there, of course; and because it is there it must have some significance. Yet it makes no difference to God seen after the old model, because for him the reality of his own self-existence is sufficient. He does not need a world; he is entirely self-contained, although he has chosen to bring into existence that which is not himself. He has done this by an act of will, but he need not have done so. The splendid phrase of St Thomas Aquinas, *bonum diffusivum sui*, 'the good diffuses or gives itself outwards', does not appear to have been taken with adequate seriousness. It *might* have been used to indicate that since God is truly good, indeed is goodness itself, and since he is also a unity in whom attributes and essence are one and the same, he cannot do other than create, and in creating expresses that essential goodness. Had this been understood, there would not have been such excessive stress on the divine self-sufficiency. Rather, there would have been a recognition that the goodness which 'diffuses itself' does this because it is of the very nature of such goodness to give in love; it would not *be* such goodness did it not both wish, and we can even say *need*, just that kind of created order for the expression of itself.

W. H. Auden says in one of his poems,

> Space is the Whom our loves are needed by,
> Time is our choice of How to love, and why.

In those beautiful words we have a statement of the way in which the world is needed if God is Love. We have also a statement of the intention for our own existence, namely that in our finitude we shall learn 'how to love' and thus learning we shall know the 'why' of it – which is God himself as the Lover who invites and welcomes responsive love from his creation.

All this helps us towards the answer to the question: what is the world's destiny? That answer can be put very briefly. The world's destiny is *in God as receptive Love*. But that answer needs to be spelled out in more detail. I shall seek to do this by speaking first about the traditional four 'last things', as the church's theologians have called them: death, judgment, heaven, and hell. Inevitably, however, the way in which these will be discussed will be different from the conventional one, precisely because the deity to whom each of them is relevant is now envisaged in a different fashion. What is more, for us the point of the so-called 'last things' must be in their immediate significance in our present experience as human beings, as men and women who have our own day-by-day existence, and not merely as indicative of what is thought will occur at some time in the near or distant future. In other words, the world's destiny and our human destiny within the world is *now*, not later on at the end of our finite existence or when the whole created order has come to some supposed termination. In modern jargon, these matters – death, judgment, heaven, hell – are existential to us and for us.

This should not suggest that the future is of no importance at all. On the contrary, it is of quite enormous importance; but to understand how this is the case we need again to remember the 'in God' stress. God himself, in his accepting and receiving and using what goes on in the world, *is that future*; the future is not something added on or extra. There is nothing which is not open to the divine acceptance and reception save evil *as evil*. And even evil, transformed into opportunity for good, can serve the purpose of God and be employed by him as a means to such good. As I have said in this book on two earlier occasions, for the Christian the paradigm for this transformation is the way in which the sheer evil of crucifixion on Good Friday is made into the sheer good manifested on Easter morning, where the Cross, hitherto the sign of degradation and shame, becomes the 'sign of victory'. That is how God acts in the world, how God is, and how God as Love makes 'even the wrath of man to turn to his praise'. Thus we see that in the future, which ultimately is nothing other than God in his receptive aspect, there is a destiny for whatever has taken place in the world, good or evil.

Let us begin with death. We all know the old saying that the only two certain facts are 'death and taxes'. Everybody is going to die and everybody should take this into reckoning when he or she is considering human existence. In many quarters today there is a conspiracy to hide the fact, associated sometimes with funeral customs; the preparation of a dead body so that it will seem to be merely sleeping, and the use of such phrases as 'passed away', 'left us' and the like, instead of frank and honest talk about somebody's *having died*. Some observers have told us that for large numbers of people today, death is the ultimate obscenity which should never be mentioned in conversation and which should be covered over and hidden so far as possible. The result of this taboo has been more than unfortunate, because it has suggested strongly that we can live quite satisfactorily without ever letting the thought of our inevitable death enter our minds or in any way effect our day-by-day existence. This is unrealistic and absurd.

The German existentialist philosopher Martin Heidegger once spoke of death as both 'the finality of life' and 'life in its finality'. By this he was urging that we should understand that we exist *towards death*, first, as the ending of our present mortal existence (indeed the very word 'mortal' says this about us), but secondly, as the inescapable terminus of our life which qualifies every moment before that event occurs. We are to live as those who know they will die. Among other things, this tells us that no one of us is absolutely indispensable in a world which will go on after our time in it; we are expendable and we should realize that this is the case. Obviously we need not spend all our time in contemplation of our going to die; that would be both absurd and unhealthy. On the other hand, the man or woman who has not taken death into account and thus included it in his or her understanding or existence is unquestionably a person who is living, or trying to live, in what is nothing other than a fool's paradise. To allow death to qualify our view of life will bring us to take that life with more seriousness, with the knowledge that since 'we shall not pass this way again' we must do the best that we can while we are here to make some contribution to our fellows and to the ongoing of the world in its creative advance.

There is another important consideration, however. That is the patent truth that we 'die daily'. Physically there is a death of the cells whose usefulness has come to an end and their replacement by new cells. In our thinking, and hence in our adjustment to the successive moments of our life, we also die to the old and must come to live in and for the new. As we grow in age, we leave behind much that has been part of our human existence. Its effects continue with us, providing from our past the material upon which we make decisions in the light of newer and different possibilities. But the person who has not died to his childish fancies or adolescent desires is commonly taken to be retarded. We are to grow up and to grow on, not to try to exist in a past which is over and done with and which cannot be preserved for ever.

When I was a child, I was given at the time of my confirmation a motto which I was told should ever be in my mind: 'For men may rise by stepping-stones of their dead selves to higher things.' These words from Alfred Lord Tennyson may seem to many today to be a little trite and hardly suitable for a child. None the less, they state a truth which deserves constant attention. If we are to move on into what the motto called 'higher things' – better adjustment, wider usefulness, more generous participation in the total human enterprise – it is necessary that we should die to the lesser self which has gone before. This is folk wisdom; it is the common sense of those who are perhaps simple and unsophisticated but who for that very reason may be gifted with a deeper insight than many a modern person who thinks himself highly intelligent and sophisticated.

We die, which is the sign of our finitude and mortality and which should be taken into our project for life. We are also 'judged'; and this brings us to the second in the traditional list of the 'last things'. It may be that the word 'judgment' is not quite satisfactory; I myself should prefer to speak of appraisal. Judgment suggests a law-court with some external agent pronouncing sentence upon those who are brought before him; while appraisal connotes an evaluation which is much more profound because it is in terms of something more truly human than the external sentence that a judge may pronounce.

For one thing, we appraise ourselves. The man or woman who is living in the most human fashion is made aware, sometimes very vividly but often through a vague feeling of dissatisfaction or discomfort, of what he or she has done that is unworthy. Only somebody who sees nothing but evil in human existence could deny that there are also times when we know ourselves to have done a useful and valuable thing, in action or in word; there is nothing to be said for a continual denigration of human choice and behaviour. But there is nothing to be said, either, for the stupidly cheerful idea that everything has always been for the best and that it would be quite improper to say to oneself, 'That was a bad thing, a mistaken choice, a selfish rather than generous act.' By what standard, then, are we to undertake this self-appraisal? Here, once again, the new model gives us an answer. We are to judge ourselves by the degree to which and the way in which we measure up to the love that is humanly possible, in the light of the divine Love that works ceaselessly in the creation and in human existence.

Not only do we appraise ourselves; we are also appraised by our fellow humans. Their opinion may be good or bad, but it is something with which we must reckon. What part have we played, how active or inactive have we been, in what way have we contributed or failed to contribute to the life of the community in which we live, to the lives of those with whom we work, to our neighbours and acquaintances, and so on and on and on? Such appraisals may not seem to count for much. Certainly, they are frequently highly prejudiced and unfair, although now and again they may be disturbing to us precisely because they have been penetrating and accurate. The criterion for judgment here is not always the same as that by which we evaluate ourselves; nevertheless there may be the possibility that it is an accurate appraisal, made with some degree of genuine objectivity. In any event, it is something which is continually with us and can make us more keenly aware of our communal relationships. In our family, perhaps, there can be a more kindly appraisal. But we need constantly to relate our own self-appraisal with that of others if we are to come anywhere near an understanding of our worth to society in all its dimensions.

There is also an appraisal made in terms of longer historical awareness. In what ways have we done our part in promoting wider good, more justice, better conditions for our fellows? That judgment is appropriate not only at the point of our death but in longer perspective. As succeeding generations remember us, if they remember us at all, how will they think about us? Here judgments are subject to considerable change. At one time the view may be that we have been incredibly stupid, lacking in insight, inadequate if not entirely useless, as others look back at us; at another time, we may be appraised as ahead of our age, persons of great insight, whose contribution has been sadly unappreciated and unrewarded. We are familiar with the way in which some historians, writing from the wisdom of hindsight, can engage in the unpleasant job of 'de-bunking' heroes; while others who also have the benefit of that hindsight can exalt those who earlier seemed insignificant or unworthy of attention. Most of those who read this book will doubtless not be in the category of such well-known personages; we have been little known and we will soon be forgotten. And yet it remains true that we have made, or have failed to make, something of ourselves in respect to what human existence at large has become. All of us have made our contribution, for good or for ill, to the way in which things have gone in the world. Probably this kind of appraisal is in terms of such criteria as righteousness, but righteousness is the way in which love is worked out in social contexts. The judgment is no more infallible and unerring than is that of our own time and place or that which we make of ourselves. But it is worthy of attention. We do not know now what later ages will have to say, if they have anything at all to say; but yet we can seek to do our job and live our lives as responsibly as possible, aware of what we are likely to have done or not done for the amelioration of existence for those who follow us.

The supreme and final appraisal, however, is what really matters. That appraisal could be stated in this way: to what degree, in what way, have I been participant in the cosmic enterprise as a whole? The contribution which I make will doubtless be very small; but has it been worthwhile? In the sight of the all-wise and all-generous cosmic Lover, how do I look? Seeing my life as a whole, with its 'ups' and 'downs', its goodness and its wrongness, what is the realistic reckoning which such a Lover may make? St John of the Cross spoke beautifully of the so-called 'final judgment': 'At the end of our days, we shall be judged by our loving.' This appraisal by God, seen as the new model portrays God, will necessarily be penetrating and comprehensive; but the criterion by which such an appraisal is made will be that self-same love which is both the divine character and the human possibility.

We move on now to 'heaven' and 'hell'. In conventional thinking these are held out as likely destinations for each human life. If a man or woman has obeyed the divine commandments and behaved in a fashion which is appropriate for human existence, there will be a final reward which is heaven. If that person has disobeyed the commandments and behaved in a less than fully human fashion, there will be punishment which is hell. I believe that here, above all, we must give an existential interpretation rather than the sort of interpretation which conventional piety has provided. What is to be said about any *post mortem* situation will be consequent upon what is said about that existential reality of heaven and hell.

Heaven, I take it, denotes the circumstances and condition of life in and with God. Hell is to be taken as the absence of such life in God, although we may well recoil from the lurid portrayal of it in much religious art and in what is often sadistic religious language. If God is nothing other than sheer Love-in-Act, we may say that when and as any man or woman has been given, if only for a brief moment, an experience of love in its profoundest sense – mutuality, giving-and-receiving, life in and with another – then there has been some glimpse of heaven. The glimpse has been partial and limited, made available for the most part through finite means. It will be the same if we are ready to grant, following what was suggested in a previous chapter, that beauty in its various forms is also a working of God, who in what he does makes known what he is. So those experiences in which we are caught up in a beauty that is so real that we feel that it cannot be made only by human hands, will be moments in which we are 'in heaven'. As I have said, all these experiences will be limited; they will not continue throughout our lives; they will be at best glimpses of a harmony, in beauty and in love, through righteousness and caring, which abides for ever. But they will be glimpses of God, even a brief and joyful sharing in God's own life.

The other side is the absence of any such experience; even more terribly, it is life lived in utter isolation, through our own choice made in such freedom as is ours. William Morris said that 'fellowship is heaven, the absence of fellowship is hell'. By that definition, most of us have spent a good deal of our time in hell. We may not have been vividly conscious of the fact, yet the truth has been that we have had hours of 'quiet desperation' when we have felt that 'through our own fault, our own grievous fault' we have denied our fellowship with God and with our human brothers and sisters. We have sought to be 'on our own', to 'go it alone'; and in consequence we have a sense of dereliction and loss. Most of us live mixed lives in this respect. We have glimpses of heaven and we have experienced hell. Such is the human condition, where actualization of our best good is always partial and where wrong is a present threat to us.

In the Catholic tradition there is another emphasis: the concept of an intermediate state short of heaven, often called purgatory. Here too we can see an existential concern. For that tradition says that none is fit for admission to heaven, save St Mary and some of the saints; the rest of us need purification or purgation from our self-centredness before we are fit to enjoy the 'beatific vision'. So we may urge that in our present experience we must undergo mortification – or a death to our self-centredness – in order to achieve sanctification or genuine blessedness. In other words, the ambiguity of our existence requires a continuing openness to the action of God if we are to become fully human 'in God's image'. In God himself, too, there could very well be an increasing reception of his children, as he remembers them in his own life and is able more and more to employ them for his own purpose. In a moment we must say more about that divine memory. Perhaps I may refer again to my recent book *After Death – Life in God* (SCM Press 1980) for further discussion about these matters, as well as for a defence of such Catholic devotions as prayers for the dead and veneration for St Mary and the other saints, to which reference is made later in this chapter.

Human existence is indeed always ambiguous. Is there anything more that can be said?

At this point the ultimate Christian assurance, confirmed by the Process insistence that God is the final recipient or affect, comes into the picture. While human existence is indeed ambiguous, the divine Lover is altogether good and 'altogether lovely', as the old phrase has it. In God there is sheer harmony. Indeed he is, in Whitehead's splendid phrase, 'the Harmony of harmonies'. Created occasions have had their moments when harmony, whether in loving or appreciation of beauty or integration of life in some just cause, has been enjoyed, if only for a brief period. In God's consequent aspect, however, those creaturely harmonies are given their due place in the total divine harmony, evaluated and graded according to their worth and in terms of their contribution to the ongoing purpose of God in the created world. They are unfailingly *remembered by God*.

The word used here, 'remember', brings us to the final point in our consideration of the world's destiny when God is seen as cosmic Love. Human memory is very partial. It is accompanied by a forgetfulness in which much that was valued is lost. At best it is but sporadic and subject to vicissitude. But God's memory is everlasting and unfailing. The divine knowledge is inclusive of all actuality which has been achieved in the creation. Nothing is forgotten, nothing is 'cast as rubbish to the void' – save evil, which is not so much cast aside as transmuted into potentiality for some other achievement of good.

In a poem from the early years of this century, the American Richard Hovey stated this in a vivid way:

> God has said, Ye shall fail and perish;
> But the thrill you have felt tonight
> I shall keep in my heart and cherish
> When the worlds have passed out of sight.

I owe this quotation to Professor Charles Hartshorne, who once used it in an admirable discussion of the infallibility of the divine memory. Whatever good we have known, which is to say whatever 'bits of heaven' have been part of our experience, whatever has been significant and valuable in our lives, whatever has been done or thought or said which is a contribution to the 'Love that moves the sun and the other stars': all this God 'keeps in his heart and cherishes'. This is objective immortality – the taking into God of the achievements in the creation. In the verse I have quoted, the reference is plainly to love shared between two humans. That is entirely right, since in that love, when it *is* love and not merely selfish or sensual gratification, God is clearly active. It is that love which gives us the key and clue to the way things really 'go' in the world and with God. And here, once more, the folk-wisdom of the human race is in agreement, although it has not commonly talked in terms of the divine reality but rather in terms of existence at its best, its most complete, and its most fulfilled.

God is the world's destiny. To be participant in God is to share in that destiny. But the question must now be asked: is this to be a *conscious* sharing, in which there will be a subjective awareness of such destiny?

Among those who accept wholeheartedly the new model of God and who share fully in the Process conceptuality used in this book, there is a difference of opinion on this question of subjective immortality. Whitehead never gave a final statement of his views. His interpreter, Professor Charles Hartshorne, has come down against the idea of subjective immortality, arguing that it is a denial of human finitude, a refusal to accept the greatness of God as Lover by insisting on our own extravagant importance, and thus in essence is self-centred and not God-centred. Two interesting essays on the subject have presented opposing positions. Professor Schubert Ogden in his 'The Meaning of Christian Hope' (published in *The Union Seminary Quarterly Review* for winter-summer 1975, a festschrift number in honour of Daniel Day Williams) argues strongly against subjective immortality, claiming that it amounts to an idolatrous assertion of selfhood over against the all-inclusive love which is God. On the other hand, Marjorie Suchocki has recently written a comment on

Ogden's position with an argument for subjective immortality; this appeared in *The Journal of Religion* for July 1977. Miss Suchocki attempts to meet Ogden's objections as not necessary implications of a Process theism, but she also goes on to urge that, in her view, only if each entity shares in an immortality which has its subjective side can the triumph of the divine Love over all evil be adequately established.

My own position is much closer to Ogden's. Yet I do not think that a Process theology need be entirely negative about the idea of subjective immortality. It may be possible to state it in such a fashion that something more like the traditional 'communion of saints', a profoundly real sharing together in the love of God, is posited, rather than a highly individualistic claim that there will be 'glory for me'. In the Process conceptuality there seems to me nothing which systematically rules out such a possibility. If all achievements which are of value are taken into God, may not the agents who have done that achieving also be sufficiently valuable to be taken into him? But I do not wish to press this point, as if the new model of God could not be maintained unless there were such an assurance. For genuinely religious purposes, the insight that the Love from which all has proceeded is the Love that will receive all seems to me to be the basic affirmation of faith in the cosmic Lover. Such a loving God will do all that is possible, in a creation like ours, for the fulfilment of those who have been made participants in the creative enterprise. Perhaps the most fitting attitude is a reverent agnosticism, coupled with a hope, never to be demonstrated in this finite world, that in some fashion we may have a share – or perhaps it is better to say that those whom we have loved may have their share – in the ultimate harmonization which is God. For myself, this need not, and as a matter of fact does not, include subjective immortality.

A practical question might be raised at this point. In the Catholic tradition through the centuries, and now among many Protestants as well, reverence for St Mary and the saints and the custom of praying for the departed have been part of the life of devotion. Can this custom have validity when the view of destiny just presented has been accepted? My answer is that it can; and for several reasons. First, if there is subjective immortality then obviously by some sort of communion with the departed, which such prayers imply, it might well be that our desire for their 'growth in God' is effectual. But second, if there is objective but not subjective immortality, if there is the reception by God of accomplishments by created occasions, we have no reason to assume that human prayers for those 'loved long since' may not open to the divine Love further possibilities for the employment of what he has received. I have insisted that creaturely acts have their effect upon the God who lovingly works with children and for the world. Hence it might well be that our prayerful remembrance of the departed gives him further opportunity to use them in his continuing activity. Thirdly and very practically, such prayer keeps the departed fresh in our own memory and is therefore effectual in urging us on to more adequate service of God and hence to greater achievement of our fulfilment in him.

There can be no question, however, that the biblical material, found in such books as Revelation, must be taken as a mythological way of asserting that *in God* all is brought to its proper fulfilment. Just as the creation tales in Genesis are a mythological way of saying that God is the source of order and novelty in the world, so the biblical talk of 'last things' in the broader context of eschatology can be seen to have the purpose of asserting that God is the final end or goal. Such myths should be 'de-mythologized', so that their true intention may be grasped by us today. Perhaps we cannot share the imagery which our ancestors gave to such an intention, but we can share their firm conviction that in God 'all shall be well'.

Two other matters may be considered in this chapter. One has to do with the non-human aspects of the creation. The other has to do with the possibility of other worlds than the one which we inhabit.

As to the former, it is not without interest that we read in scripture about 'a new heaven and *a new earth*', in connection with the ultimate destiny of this creation. For far too long a time, more especially I think since the Reformation focussed attention almost exclusively on human sin and salvation, we have been the victims of a wilful neglect of the natural realm. Discussion seems always to have centred on *human* experience and *human* history, as if the world of nature, apart from that human side, were only a stage-setting for the really important concerns of God. But it is to be noted that in the Bible nature is not dismissed so readily; it is of value in itself because it is of value to God. Now that we are aware of the intimate relationship of human existence with nature in its wider sense, seeing that human life has emerged from that natural order and (despite its novel and distinctive quality) still remains part of that order, we should be the more prepared to believe that in the working out of the divine intention, nature must have its place and play its part. It must also share in the destiny which is the reality of God in his receptivity. How this may be accomplished we do not know. How could we? But we may note that the Eastern Orthodox churches stress this value of the natural order. They are far less anthropocentric than Western Christians both in respect to creation and also in the matter of 'salvation'.

Indeed they are prepared to speak of 'cosmic redemption'. Perhaps we can learn from them and move away from our excessive stress on what *we* humans are, what *we* may do, what *we* may become, how *we* are valued, and learn to see ourselves in a more natural, even cosmic, context.

Yet it is to be remembered that ours is not the only conceivable world. In an appended note to an earlier chapter, this was mentioned. This leads to the second point: other worlds. It is implicit in the model of God as creative and responsive and receptive Love that he shall have *a* world; otherwise we should be talking of creatorhood without creation, response when there might be nothing to which response was made, and reception of that which was not there to be received. But it need not be *this* world – this world which has its particular style, its observable regularities, its own special characteristics. There is no reason to assume that this world which we ourselves know has exhausted the divine creativity, responsiveness, and receptivity. If God is genuinely inexhaustible, with infinite resources, he may very well have other worlds in which to be active creatively and redemptively. The present world-order seems to be running down; it is in the grip of entropy. Could there not be a succeeding one for further cosmic adventure in love? Or even, as a daring hypothesis, may there not even now be other worlds alongside this one, where God is engaging in other adventures and where, as in this one, the purpose is 'amorization'? If so, the one and only destiny for each and all of them will be in God himself, as for our world and for our human existence he is the one and only supreme and final destiny. All is *ad majorem dei gloriam*, in the famous Jesuit phrase.

12

The Church as the Community of Love

When the material in this book was first delivered as lectures, one of my students at St John's University pointed out to me something that previously I had not noticed. She remarked that the various beliefs about the nature and purpose of the Christian community, the church, could be correlated with the model of God which its leaders had held or were still holding. Since my student said this, I have frequently thought how illuminating that can be. I begin this chapter with a consideration of this significant point.

Suppose that the model for God is taken to be the absolute dictator. In that case, it is highly likely that those who believe this will look at the church in what is nowadays called a 'triumphalist' fashion. It will be claimed that the church is the agency which controls the lives of its members, so that the hierarchy – those in positions of high authority – should regard themselves as the commissioned officers of an army. Their word will be final; they will expect obedience from the ordinary members of the community, just as a general expects obedience from the enlisted men who serve under him.

Or suppose that the model for God is what Whitehead styled 'the ruthless moral tyrant'. Then it is likely that the Christian community will be seen as the agency whose chief concern is the enforcement of a moral code, usually set forth in a series of directives about human behaviour. Again obedience will be expected. Those who disobey will be subject to penalties of one sort or another, with the ultimate sanction of excommunication or dismissal from membership.

If the model for God is a highly masculine one, marked by an aggressive quality which finds little or no place for the gentler side which stereotypically we associate with the feminine in our experience, the church will be male-centred and entirely patriarchal. What is more, it is likely that women will be put in a lower place than men; their role will be important in a 'helping' capacity but they will not be given a position equal to that accorded to members of the male sex. One may wonder if something of this attitude is not secretly present in the violent opposition, so often found in recent days, to the possibility of women serving in the church's ordained ministry. God as primarily 'father' will seem to require that it be those of 'his own gender' who act as the official agents in the ministering work of the Christian fellowship, above all in those aspects of ministering which are taken to be essential to the community's existence – like the celebration of the sacraments.

And again, to give but one more illustration, when God is seen as chiefly concerned with the maintenance of the *status quo*, the probability is that the church will be regarded as primarily interested in the preservation of 'the old ways', while new ideas, patterns of worship, and moral teaching will be dismissed as not only mistaken but probably as blasphemous denials of the divine purpose in the world. The Christian community will increasingly take the role of the angry reactionary who thinks that anything new, in whatever aspect of human life, is dangerous and should be rejected because of the threat it poses to those who wish to remain safely in the established routine.

When God is modelled after love, there is of course the opposite danger which must be avoided at all costs. Often love is assumed to be sentimental and over-tolerant. Then the church may be taken as an altogether too kindly 'grandmother' figure, making no demands and prepared to go along with whatever seems attractive and interesting. But we have insisted in this book that the sort of love which is to be predicated of God is a demanding as well as a gracious reality. That love can be severe precisely because it is merciful. It expects the best of each of its beloved and will never rest content with cheap and easy acquiescence in 'anything that goes'. In any event, the model of God as cosmic Lover will produce at its best a view of Christian fellowship which is much more human and humane than those other models which have a narrowing and confining affect.

In our discussion we have stressed the divine Love and the divine Lover. It is now desirable to see how that model must be reflected and expressed in the community of men and women who have been caught up into a response to God through the impact upon them of the witness to the event of Christ – the event in which, as I have so frequently urged, the divine Love is enacted in a definitive fashion, with its own speciality and specificity.

The biblical material which tells us of the early days of the Christian church, quite as much as the Process perspective which in this book we have been defending, makes it necessary to see that community as a dynamic and living reality; it is indeed a 'social process' and must be understood as such. Once this attitude has been adopted, many of the troublesome problems that have arisen when differing Christian groups put their emphasis on supposedly established historical positions will be resolved – or if not resolved will be seen in a different light and with sufficient flexibility to allow of adjustment and accommodation of differences. Vatican II said that the Christian church is both 'a pilgrim church' and open to continuing 'reformation' as the situations in which it finds itself introduce new factors and require new ways of seeing things. The notion that the church is a monolithic organization can then give place to the conviction that it is much more an organic affair. Legalistic ways of seeing its functioning can be rejected, and in their place can come a realization that the 'mystical Body of Christ' is best understood in vital, not mechanical, terms. When such an approach becomes the accepted and normal way of interpreting the church, every aspect of its life and mission will be seen in a new light. The implementation of all this will take time, to be sure; but there is certain to be a new realization of the ancient conviction that the Christian community is neither an army under the control of ecclesiastical officials nor a static institution, but rather is the pilgrim fellowship of those who share in a loving relationship with God known through Christ and who live so far as they are able in charity with their brothers and sisters. Thus they will demonstrate the truth of Tertullian's famous saying, but without the cynicism that many moderns feel when they hear it, that the world can see 'how these Christians love one another'.

The Process conceptuality's understanding of the world is indeed highly relevant to what we affirm about the church. I have stressed that ours is a world in process, with a general continuity which yet permits the emergence of novelty. In this world God is not the absolute, impassible, self-contained first cause or principle of being, but is the living, active, caring, related, unsurpassable (yet self-surpassing) causal and receptive agency who is to be adored because he is sheer Love-in-Act. The basic constituents of the cosmos are not things but events, 'becomings' or moments of experience; and what a given occasion *is* will always be known through what that occasion *does*. Finally, such energy-events are not 'windowless monads' but are mutually affected and affective. Ours is a *social* process.

I have also argued that Christian faith affirms that the reality we call God, around us and supporting us, is revealed to us actively in the event to which we refer when we use the name of Jesus Christ. This disclosure is so important and decisive that it makes an enormous difference, although that event is not absolutely unique in the sense that it is totally alien to what God is up to elsewhere in the creation. It is the representation, the focal and classical instance, of the divine activity everywhere. And the whole is a matter of love. For God *is* Love; and really to be grasped by this Love as it comes to us humans through finite media is to be brought to respond to it and to seek to live in terms of it, to be on the way to a truly human existence which is 'in love' because in the end it is 'in Love' – in God who himself is Love; and hence all loving relationship is a participation, however imperfect, in God's life.

In this interpretation, the Christian church is the community of those who have been bound together through sharing in the divine Love, brought near and made available in the event of Christ. It came into existence as a response to the fact of Christ and it exists as witness to the continuing experience of fellowship in him. It is in this community that the particular response of this or that person is made effective and real, since no human life is 'an island entire unto itself' but is part of a common human existence. To be human is to be part of what the Old Testament text calls 'a bundle of life'; we live together, we belong together, and we are made human together. Thus it is in the fellowship of men and women, knit together in unity by their common response to the fact of Christ, that Christian faith and worship, like Christian discipleship, can find their best expression and can be brought to their fullest flower.

St Paul has told that 'we are members one of another'; and such shared membership is made possible because those who are within it have somehow been grasped by the impact made upon them by Jesus – still felt as present with us. There is participation in what the same apostle calls 'life in Christ': *en Christo* is the Greek phrase which in his authentic writings he employs perhaps a hundred times in various contexts. This kind of life is 'a new creation', as St Paul also says, since it has come into existence as a novelty which is the result of the historical fact of Christ himself. It has been continued down the centuries through the ongoing community of the church, but we must not *identify* the church, in the sense just indicated, with the particular institutional aspects with which we are familiar or even with any specific established organization. As Vatican II said, the church *subsists* in these institutions and organizational expressions. For while nobody can be a Christian in the sense of living 'in Christ' without being in the church in the wider sense, many who are 'in Christ' may not in fact 'belong' to the sociologically defined institution commonly known as 'the church'. To put it in another way, untold numbers of men and women have been grasped by the present reality of Jesus Christ as an historical figure and as present in contemporary experience, a grasping made possible because a specific stream of life in the more general process of history is marked by its 'remembering Jesus' and in some fashion experiencing Jesus 'in the Spirit'. Yet these people are not necessarily included in statistics of 'church membership' and quite probably do not 'go to church' very frequently, if at all.

Because of this plain fact, among others, we must be on guard lest we fall into static or mechanical ways of thinking about the Christian community. As I have urged, the community is a 'social process', vital and dynamic. It is also a changing reality even though it is given a specific identity, like every other process in the cosmos, because of its continuing response to the historical event from which it took its origin. But this is not to say that it is confined to what *we* call 'the churches'.

In a Process view of things, every movement or direction proper to this or that particular occasion is *from* the past, *in* the present, and *towards* the future. So also with the church as a 'social process'. The past is remembered. Here we see the place of the biblical record, whose significance is in telling us 'how we got this way'. The remembered past is made available to us in the present through the 'proclamation of the Word' about Jesus Christ, through the celebration of the sacraments, especially the Eucharist, and through the witness of Christian discipleship to the personalized principle of life which is 'the love of God in Christ Jesus our Lord'. The historical past is thus made alive in the present moment. This is *anamnesis* or memory; not the kind of memory in which we look back wistfully to some far-distant occurrence, but the Jewish kind of memory in which what has once happened is re-experienced here and now. And the future is constantly in view, for the Christian fellowship looks forward to and labours for the kingdom of God. Its task is not to 'bring in the kingdom' through human effort, as old-fashioned liberalism used to assume; rather, it is to 'prepare and make ready the way', so that *God* can give or bring in his kingdom. The word 'kingdom' is used in the scriptures to point to God's 'sovereign rule'; it refers to the state of affairs in which God 'reigns' and is joyfully accepted as 'reigning'. Since God is the cosmic Lover, he reigns *in love*; hence talk of the kingdom of God is a way of pointing towards the situation in which such love, divine in the first instance and human by response to God, everywhere prevails. For us this is a hope; but the hope is anticipated and foreshadowed by the 'signs' that in the Bible are called 'the powers of the age to come', signs which are occasional glimpses and a partial experience of what in God is realized and made actual in its full glory.

All three tenses, then, past and present and future, must be given due place. They must also be held in balance. All are necessary to the full-orbed reality of the Christian community when that reality is properly grasped. For the church to dwell in the past alone, without regard for the present or future, will reduce Christianity to an archaeological curiosity. To dwell in the present alone, to the exclusion of the past and the future, will lead to the cult of the merely contemporary. To dwell in the future alone, without attention to the past and the present, will allow the church the luxury of unrealistic idealism. Each of the three requires the other two; each of them is qualified by the other two. This is the case with every entity or occasion in the cosmos; and it is pre-eminently the case in social processes such as the church.

We can spell this out more precisely by seeing how our existence in the church is exactly such a social process. That which is given us from the past must be prehended or grasped in a manner appropriate to our present situation or condition. The 'historic faith', for example, is continually to be 'up-dated', as Pope John XXIII insisted when he spoke of *aggiornamento*, the Italian word for 'bringing up to date'. This should not suggest that the past is being negated or minimized but rather that it is being given expression in a fashion which is relevant to our own time. Present adaptation is the outgrowth of the past, not something 'brand-new' and 'reeking of the spur of the moment', as a friend of mine once put it. The past is valued in the present; and the present is taking its direction towards the future. Yet that future is not the denial of what God has given or done in the past nor of what he is giving or doing in the present. For God the cosmic Lover is always faithful to his single purpose of Love-in-action; and the kingdom of God, for which the community looks, is the actualizing of that one abiding purpose; life in sovereign Love in a created order caught up into and made responsive to God as precisely such Love.

The task of the church is to live in such Love, so far as this can be done in a finite world. Its members are called to share in that Love and to manifest its reality in their daily living. Its boundaries cannot be defined as precisely as our little human minds, with their lust for tidiness, might wish. The fellowship spills over, so to say. There are many who seem not to belong to what St Augustine called the 'visible church' but who yet are participant in the 'invisible church'; their membership is known, not to us, but to God. In the pious phrase, while they may not be listed on any register of institutional membership, their 'names are enrolled in heaven'.

Discussion of the Christian church must include the ordained ministry of the community. Obviously every Christian has a part to play in the broad ministry of the church, in its service to God's children for the enrichment of their lives and the fulfilment of their human possibility. But because it exists in *this world of time and space* and must function within it, the fellowship requires designated persons who representatively serve both church and world in a special manner. Somebody must be primarily concerned with proclamation of the word, celebration of the sacraments, and shepherding of the people. The ordained ministry is for this purpose. But it is primarily a ministry of function and not of status. When the world is thought to be made up of fixed entities, each with its supposedly static existence, a conception of ministry can very well be held in which ordination not only places this or that person in a particular function, but also gives this or that person a position which in some fashion is ontologically different from that of others. But if we do not see the world in that way, talk of ministry in terms of status makes no sense. For that matter, it was not held in the New Testament period either, since at that time the ordained person (although the phrase was not used) did not stand apart from the church nor 'speak at' the church. The ordained person acted *for* the church; such a one was its representative in the wider and more inclusive ministering on God's behalf to its own membership and to the world in which it existed.

Negatively, a functional conception demands that we reject notions about a separation of priest and people, of ordained and unordained. It also demands that we reject the frequently-held modern idea that there is no distinction between them. Positively, it requires a view of ministry which sees that in a social process like the church there must be designated agencies with specific responsibilities, so that the whole social process may be enabled to go forward in an orderly way. God is not the God of confusion but of order, as the New Testament says. The Christian fellowship, under God, must have its 'holy order', which is a precondition for its having also what in Christian history have come to be styled 'holy orders'. We may not be very happy about some of the possible implications of that phrase; but at least it indicates that there are diverse functions within the total fellowship which is 'the Body of Christ', and that these funtions are integral to the proper functioning of the body. An ordained minister or priest is neither somebody who simply happens at a given time to lead the community's worship or in some other way act for it; nor is he – and we may hope eventually she – a person who is separated from the fellowship of Christian believers and acts upon it as if from the outside. The priest is one who is 'set apart', as the conventional phrase has it, and thereby authorized by the community to represent it and to stand for and function on its behalf in those responsibilities which cannot readily be undertaken by the community as a whole. The ordained minister is the agent of the community, not a substitute for the community. He or she is participant in the total ministry of the church, but with distinctive work to do on behalf of that ministry. In this sense, the priest is an agent of Christ himself, who is Lord of the church and its indwelling life and for whom and in whom the church acts in the world.

There is truth in the idea of 'succession', but not if that suggests the requirements of a mechanical connection or some precise and unalterable mode of ordination, nor if it implies the mere repetition of traditional formulae. Succession has its significance in that it indicates and conveys the historical continuity of the community through the maintenance of the abiding functions of proclamation, celebration, and shepherding, along with witnessing – whatever may be the particular names which are chosen to describe these identifying factors in the social process which is the church. If the past is to be efficacious in the present, the present to be an opportunity for decision in the use of that past, and the future to be in continuity with what has gone before, then the significance of succession is evident. We live *from* it; but we do not live *by* it. What, then, is required in every age is a continuation of the same modes of functioning, with the declaration of the fact of Christ, the celebration of his coming, and the care of God's children. This is the basic meaning of succession. It guarantees to us participation in the same historically grounded social process; it provides the identity of its life in Christ; and it gives us a sense of belonging to a living and growing historical reality whose roots are in the past, whose aim is towards a fulfilment in the future, and whose present existence is in the presentness of Jesus Christ himself.

In such a context, there need be no fear that attempts to find newer and (one hopes) better ways of stating the gospel for our own age will lead us astray, since the basic allegiance is not to formulae, however ancient and valuable, but to the facts of experience and the experience of facts to which those formulae point. Nor need there be worry when new modes of worship are adopted, since it is not the inherited liturgical forms that matter but the making-present through worship, above all in sacrament, of the reality of Jesus Christ, responded to and witnessed by the community. In respect to Christian discipleship with its moral imperatives, the plain fact that 'new occasions teach new duties', with consequent new ways of understanding Christian witness, makes necessary various changes that may indeed be startling to those enamoured of the old ways, but none the less are ways which are loyal to the abiding reality of Love-in-Act.

The Christian community is a living enterprise, in and under the Love that is God; it answers to the vitalities and varieties of human experience in any age. Often enough the 'old ways' are good ways and need only some re-furbishing. Yet time and again the Christian church must reckon with the danger that it may get so devoted to the past that it is unable to move ahead. And moving ahead need not be an aping of contemporary fashion; it can and should be cooperation with God in the world, as he does what Isaiah says is characteristic of him: 'I do a new thing, says the Lord God'. The Christian confidence is, or ought to be, in the God who is indeed doing 'new things' in the world – 'new things' which are also in accordance with the thing that our faith knows he has done once for all in Christ, taken as the clue or key to our understanding of the divine purpose in creation. The trouble with static views of the Christian church, surely, is that they fail to keep up with God, not that they lack an immediate appeal in any given period.

The conviction that the Christian church is a social process, informed by the life of him who lived and died and is now alive in the community called after his name, rests back finally upon the certainty that the Holy Spirit is 'the Lord and Life-giver', as the Nicene creed affirms. The Holy Spirit will 'lead us into all truth'; but truth is never static nor is it exhaustively contained in formulae. We are to '*do* the truth', St John's Gospel tells us. Truth is always a *doing*. And, as everywhere in the cosmos, what something does is what that something is. Truth is doing in faith; at its root, truth is the reality of God himself.

The charismatic revival, which is seen today in all parts of Christendom, is to be welcomed because it stresses this living, active, and present reality of God's working. Sometimes its manifestations seem overly emotional and subjective. That is to be regretted and corrected. Yet 'the Spirit gives life', as St Paul writes; and one of the reasons for the dullness and deadness of so much ecclesiastical business, so many church services, and so many local parishes, is that the Spirit has been forgotten in an over-zealous concern to maintain 'the letter'. We badly need a new awareness of the presence and power of the Spirit within the church. Perhaps one of the ways in which the Spirit may be recognized and his imperative followed is through our readiness to accept the new and Galilean model. A model of God which presents him as 'being itself', or 'first cause', or 'the absolute', or impassible and immutable reality, is a denial of the vitality of life found in the Spirit. But once the new model has been accepted, with its centring of everything in the reality of God as cosmic Lover – active and related, unfailingly at work in the world, concerned not only to preserve order but to introduce novelty – a change can come about. Of course this model must be theologically developed, liturgically expressed, and given its central place in moral teaching and discipleship:we may then expect that these 'dry bones' will come to life. I have seen this renewal in places where the new model has been made central in parochial life and other institutional groups. God as cosmic Love is not dead; he is very much alive. The church can share in that life.

As social process or the continuing movement of life in God's Love made available through the event of Jesus Christ, the church has what used to be called 'a missionary purpose', an 'apostolate'. In fact its existence *is* mission. That is to say, having regard for the original meaning of the words 'mission' and 'apostle', it is *sent to do a job*. What is that job? It is to bring Christ to all the world; or, to bring all the world to Christ. What does that mean, however? There was a time when it could be defined in terms of evangelism alone, with the proclamation of Jesus to 'heathen lands' and the urgent desire to convert the non-Christian peoples of the world to faith in him. There can still be that side of mission. But mission is rightly seen nowadays as involving primarily what has been described as 'finding Christ already present and already at work in the non-Christian world' and helping others to identify him there.

Various ways have been suggested for making this important point. Some have spoken of the pervasive and universal work of the *Logos*, or 'expressive Word of God' in other religions, indeed whenever life is enhanced and creative freedom is experienced. Some have talked about what Quakers have called '*that* of God' in the depths of every human existence. John Cobb has lately said that all instances of 'creative transformation' are the work of God, in that mode or aspect of his activity which we Christians find focussed in Jesus of Nazareth and his work in the specific culture of which we are a part. All these suggestions are helpful. But for myself I should wish to stress particularly the phrase from the old Roman Catholic liturgy for Holy Week which I have quoted earlier in this book: *ubi caritas et amor ibi Deus* – 'where love and concern are seen, there God is'. I urge that we are found of God, and in our response we find him when there is a release in any time or place of the love that God *is*. To say that is to say that where there is genuine loving action, in all its richness, God is indeed at work.

Hence the church's mission is to help others identify this loving action and this Love-in-Act, whatever may be the many different garbs which it may wear. In truth it is nothing other than the secret heart of things, or what I have styled the basic thrust and drive in the cosmos. Insofar as this is known, experienced and shared, men and women are on the way to what the Jewish-Christian tradition has spoken about under the word 'salvation'; it is wholeness of life, abundant life, *shalom*, human becoming in love and as love. That includes concern about justice, liberation from oppression, and struggle for human equality of opportunity and growth. In its fullness, it is entrance into 'life eternal', as St John's gospel puts it; it is 'life which is life indeed'.

The Christian church must relate all this to the man of Nazareth, since for the church that man is the focal and decisive human representation of what the cosmic Love is always acting and working for. This requires that the Christian message, as well as the church which bears it, can never be isolated from the yearnings and desires, the fulfilments and release, made available in any religion or culture. Yet with all due recognition of the pluralism which prevails in the religious quest and religious discovery in so many different places and times, there is no need for negation of the specific Christian affirmation. We are brought always to the point of sharing with others, even in what used to be thought of as alien religions, that which we ourselves have experienced in Christ, just as we are also to be open to receive from others their own particular insights.

On an earlier page I quoted from a recent book by a French priest, Paul Guèrin. I wish now to quote another passage from the same book (*I Believe*, p. 54), a passage which has specific christological intention. Guèrin uses the analogy of love, which he rightly sees as the most helpful to us:

> The purpose of love, at least in intention, is to be the other without ceasing to be oneself and without preventing the other from being himself. There can be no love if the distance is not maintained; it is essential to be two and really different if love is to exist . . . But love is my giving of myself in such a way that the other is yet supported and nourished by me. If we will fill out the statements 'You are my wife' and 'You are my husband', we get something like this: 'I, the man who loves you, have allowed you to be fully a woman. I, the woman who loves you, have enabled you to be fully

a man. You are the woman in me; you are the man in me. Another self, or rather an other self.'

In those words of Guèrin we have stated what an ancient Christian prayer styled *admirabile commercium*, 'wonderful exchange', in which the divine Lover and the human lover-in-the-making live each in the other. I have quoted in another chapter the Johannine words, 'I am in the Father and the Father in me.' So Jesus is made to say; hence he can also say in the same gospel, 'The Father and I are one.' What in Jesus is achieved, according to Christian faith, is not a total anomaly; it is the supreme instance or the decisive case, with relevance for all men and women everywhere.

The mission of the Christian church then is to interpret the experience of such profound loving, wherever it may be found, as nothing other and nothing less than the bringing into fellowship of the cosmic Lover and the human lover-being-made; and to interpret this with a vital realization of what it signifies. The speciality of the event of Christ vividly enacts this unitive reality and placards it before the world. Thus it confirms and corrects, rather than rejects or negates, any such experience found in non-Christian places. In our dialogue with others we may confidently trust that Christ's decisive role will be enhanced and validated, just as he himself enhances and validates the divine-human meeting to which other religious traditions in their own fashion may also bear their responsible witness.

13

Faith and the New Model

A final and vital question remains for us to consider. How do we come to believe in, accept, and relate our own existence to this new model? Granted that it is a more acceptable model than the old one, granted that it makes more sense of the biblical material and can more readily fit into our knowledge of the world and of ourselves, granted that a case can be made for it as pointing more adequately to the character of God as the basic thrust and drive in the world, we have then to ask what is the appropriate attitude to God as disclosed in the event of Christ? In other words, we must consider the nature of religious faith, for it is only in faith and by faith that this model – or any other, for that matter – can come alive in our lives.

What is faith?

For a great many people today, it appears that faith is simple credulity. It is not quite the same as Alice's Queen speaking about believing 'impossible things before breakfast'; none the less, for many it is an attempt to say what cannot be said because there is no way in which it can be demonstrated. Kirsopp Lake, theologian and New Testament scholar of the earlier part of this century, once said that 'faith is not belief in spite of evidence but life in scorn of consequence'. I think that we must accept what this remark is getting at. But for the moment I say only that, unfortunately, it seems to a not inconsiderable number today, who would call themselves agnostics, that religious people do indeed believe 'in spite of evidence'. For such agnostics faith is an impossibility.

One of the difficulties here, of course, is that faith, defined as they probably define it, is the acceptance of certain statements – we may call them 'propositions' – which are held up for such acceptance. Faith is thought to be primarily a matter of intellectual assent, although these critics would say that it is much more likely to be a sacrifice of intellectual respectability and a failure in intellectual honesty. It is too bad that the word 'faith' and the related word 'belief' seem thus to be identified when the latter (belief) is taken to be just that kind of non-intellectual activity. Historically, however, the word faith has had a wider and indeed a different meaning. We must explore this in a moment.

In many circles much has been made of the distinction between 'belief that . . .' and 'faith in . . .'. While the distinction can be pressed so far that it sometimes looks as if there were to be no intellectual content whatsoever when faith is in view, there is truth in the insistence that faith, in the profoundly religious sense in which believers have commonly meant it, is much more a matter of 'faith in . . .' and usually is faith *in a person*. Obviously that person must exist or else *any* attitude towards him or her would be silly. Yet the important aspect of faith for religious people is not that God exists, although this is taken to be the case; rather, it is that the God who does indeed exist is such that commitment to him, engagement with him, and willed response to him, are both meaningful and important.

A further point may be made here by citing a significant distinction (found in St Thomas Aquinas and also other Catholic theologians) between *fides qua creditur* and *fides quae creditur*. By the former, these Christian thinkers have intended to indicate the act of faith or our commitment and dedication to God as he has disclosed himself in Jesus Christ and elsewhere in human experience; by the latter, they have intended to speak about the tradition, embodied in creeds or other formulations, which over the centuries has developed as a way of affirming in verbal form exactly what and who it is to which or whom such active faith or commitment and dedication is directed. Unhappily, ambiguity of language has often led to a disastrous mistake, whereby many have been led to assume that these two meanings of faith are identical. But of course they are not. A simple Christian man or woman, who knows very little about *the* faith, may very well have more *faith* – more self-surrender to God in responsive commitment – than the wisest of theologians. As St Ambrose put it, *non in dialectica complacuit deo salvum facere populum suam*: 'it was not in "dialectic" that God has been pleased to save his people'. This was one of Cardinal Newman's favourite quotations; and rightly so.

In one sense faith as commitment is not demonstrable; it is not like the concern to prove things about triangles or the behaviour of quanta of energy. But, on the other hand, it is not irrational, nor does it ask for acceptance of what may very well not be true at all. I recall a picture on the cover of a small pamphlet which was published by the ministry commission of a Christian denomination in the United States; it urged young people to consider the possibility of offering themselves for the ministry of the church. The picture showed a young man standing on the diving-board of a swimming pool. Underneath it were the words, 'Ministry is a great adventure of faith.' But alas! those who produced the pamphlet had not realized that there was no water in that swimming-pool. My own comment about it was, 'If that's how it is, then ministry is not an adventure of faith but damned foolishness.'

This silly story has its serious side. No invitation to faith and no act of faith on anyone's part can make sense if there is not some reason to assume that it has to do with what is genuinely the case. We must have *some* grounds which are valid (even if only broadly indicative and suggestive) for our thinking that God *is* before we can reasonably be asked to have faith in that God.

In the earlier chapters of this book, I have attempted to show that the new model of God is in contact with things as they really are and as they really go. I have urged that philosophically, scientifically, and religiously, as well as existentially, and in terms of human experience as ordinary people know it, there is much to be said for conceiving or imaging the basic cosmic thrust and drive in the fashion which the new model suggests. In other words, I have sought to make a reasonable case for God's existence in terms which the model of cosmic Lover intimates. I have spoken of the way in which Process Thought makes such a model possible and I have said that the general line of biblical teaching, when taken intelligently and imaginatively and not literally and unhistorically, requires that we think of God, if we think of him at all, in some such fashion. I have noted that God, so understood, is actively at work in the creation, disclosing himself under finite conditions and inviting a response from his human children.

One could say all this and one could accept it as a more satisfactory explanation of how things are and go in the world than one which rejects all notions of deity and attempts to interpret the world and what is in it from a strictly non-theistic or even firmly atheistic perspective. But there is a difference between intellectual agreement and vital religious existence, between assent to a theoretical world-view and the dedication or commitment of life to that reality about which the world-view speaks.

I have used the word 'commitment' – a word that has come into currency in recent years as a way of describing faith. To commit oneself is to give oneself, to the limit to which one is able, to another person. When we speak in this fashion, we are affirming that the way in which we relate ourselves to God is through placing our trust and confidence in the active loving which we have seen disclosed in the world – and for Christians supremely and decisively disclosed in the event of Jesus Christ. In committing oneself to God, disclosed in that place and through that event which occurred in Palestine at a given time in history, we are 'in faith'.

To take that attitude, at first perhaps tentatively but as time goes on more and more firmly, is to open oneself to a new possibility. It is to be ready to accept the disclosure of God as Love there and then; and it can lead on to a deepening discernment that such Love is at work elsewhere and always. In other words, we are not in the situation where (as I have observed earlier) we presume to say that the event of Christ *confines* God's Love, but rather we say that it *defines* it, so that we can acknowledge its presence and power in other places and other times.

To have such faith is not a purely individual matter, although unfortunately there have been some Christians who have talked as if it were. Certainly each one of us must be 'in faith' if it is to have any cutting-edge. But we come to such faith largely because there is a long history of commitment which is embodied in the ongoing Christian community. My own commitment, my own trust and confidence, may not be very strong; yet I can rest back upon the witness of the community and let it support me in my weaker moments. Nor could I ever have known that such commitment was possible if there had not been a community which proclaimed it, which lived by it, and which was concerned to make it available.

Having said this, I must go on to urge that we are always in danger of confusing the church's enduring faith with the church's formulation of that faith. We have seen that in the Middle Ages a distinction was made, by St Thomas Aquinas among others, between *fides quae creditur* and *fides qua creditur*. The former means *the* faith which is believed, the latter faith *by which* one believes. By omitting the definite article in the second instance, I have sought to indicate that we are there dealing with precisely the commitment which this or that one of us, inspired by the continuing witness of the Christian fellowship, is enabled to make to God active in the world and decisively active in Jesus Christ. It was this commitment which led to formulations of the faith – *fides quae creditur*.

Yet here once more we must make a distinction. For it is not so much the precise definitions of 'the faith' which are significant, but the deep and usually unspoken although profoundly felt and experienced conviction, as a matter of lived fact, which has brought about a kind of living 'in faith', which in its turn has led to increasing discernment of God's loving concern for his children in every place, and which eventually requires some propositional statement to express those convictions and safeguard that discernment. The reason for such a statement is obvious. Human existence is at least partially rational; hence we want and we must seek to develop a form of words which, although always less than adequate, is much better than our remaining entirely silent about what is so important to us.

So we come back to the new model. If 'coming to God' is possible only by the initial act of faith and then the repeated acting in faith of which I have spoken, it is inevitable that we shall wish to speak about it. How can we do this? We cannot do it in thought-forms which are damaging to the concrete reality of life lived in trust in the Love that is God. Nor can we do it in words that suggest false ideas of God and his manner of working; nor use language that is quite irrelevant in our own day. Surely none of these will do. Rather, we must find images, pictures, symbols – in a word, a model – which are true to the commitment, which do not negate the reality of religious life, and which are in meaningful relationship to whatever else we may know. Here the new model has its special value. For it is true to the commitment of trust and confidence in a divine Love that holds us in its grasp; it is in accordance with the human experience of such Love-in-action in a world of tragedy yet of promise; and it has its partial confirmation in the rest of our human knowledge.

We should always remember, however, the second part of the quotation from Kirsopp Lake, with which I began this chapter: that faith is 'life in scorn of consequence'. In the sense in which he must have intended it, that phrase tells us that to live in trust and confidence in cosmic Love is no promise of an easy life without risk, without challenge and without a call to adventure. On the contrary, it is demanding of our best effort and of our willingness to risk everything; it is a call to us to respond to the highest and best we can conceive. Above all, it is a requirement that we use *our imagination*.

The nineteenth century German theologian, Albrecht Ritschl, overstated the matter when he spoke of faith as a 'value-judgment' rather than what he called an 'existential judgment' – by which, in his own fashion, he was speaking about what I should call ontological statements. What he was getting at might be phrased otherwise and better by saying that we can only affirm things ontological – which is to say, things that have to do with the deepest cosmic reality and which sum up generalizations drawn from immediate intuitions and insight – when we have first of all been prepared to do what John Keats urged was the clue to human living, to 'trust the heart's affections'. In other words, we need to put our reliance not on logical exercises but on the most profound of our 'feeling-tones', upon the imaginative and appreciative capacity which speaks from our hearts and to our hearts. If God *is* Love and if therefore the best model for God is cosmic Lover, that attitude or posture is only to be expected. For Love speaks to love, Lover speaks to beloved, God's heart speaks to human hearts. Cardinal Newman's motto has it right; *cor ad cor loquitur*. Only the one who has learned to love, however imperfectly that may be, can have faith in God as Love.

To some people this may sound sentimental. I am convinced that it is stark truth – very uncomfortable to our little human hearts, to be sure, but inescapable if we are to move on towards our high human calling to become created lovers, in the image of the one in whom the divine Love was supremely enacted 'for us men and for our wholeness'.

A final point is relevant to this discussion. It has to do with 'verification' by the finding of 'referents' to which appeal may be made in order to give a grounding in experience and observation to our assertions about God. One of the complaints made by followers of 'positivism' and modern linguistic thought is that religious people and *a fortiori* theologians constantly make statements for which no demonstration is possible in terms of concrete fact. This charge may have some justification in respect to the kind of talk which led to the establishment of the old model for deity. In that talk, the only possible reference and hence the only means for verification would seem to have been – at least for much theological assertion of this type – logic of a deductive variety. To be sure, this is not a fair judgment when we come to see the way in which for instance St Thomas Aquinas tries to ground a good deal of his theologizing on the factual reality of the phenomenal world, as well as on the data provided by God's self-revelation reported in the Bible. But there is sufficient truth in the charge for many to think that the theological enterprise is largely a construction of the human mind in its desire to build up a picture of the world and of God which will be logically satisfying, but which makes little concrete appeal to the actual experience of men and women in the ordinary world.

The approach which has been set forth in this book and which is accepted by those of us who subscribe to the Process conceptuality is quite different. Essentially it is by way of generalization from what is concretely known and humanly experienced. In this procedure, we begin with an analysis of what it 'feels like' to be human and what we actually observe in the world about us. The categories which are suggested by such study are then applied to ever wider areas and an effort is made to discover whether these categories do, or do not, accord with such further data as may come within our range of knowledge, and hence require interpretation. If they do not fit, they must be discarded; if they do fit, although perhaps not as neatly as precise minds might desire, they are so far forth to be trusted and employed for continuing interpretation.

But no claim is made in Process thinking that these categories are absolute, final, and entirely incorrigible. On the contrary, we have here what Whitehead, as we have seen, preferred to call 'a vision of reality' – a portrayal of the cosmic advance as a whole – which is suggestive, illuminating, and useful for our developing understanding. Instead of clear and distinct ideas reached through severely logical argument, we have intimations of truth, with a vivid centre of assured fact, but with nuances and shadings as we continue our interpretive efforts. Logic is valuable and must always be used so far as it is appropriate; but what I have styled 'feeling-tones', evaluation, appreciation, and aesthetic awareness and response, are also of the greatest significance and cannot be overlooked or minimized. 'The heart has its reasons', Pascal said, 'that the reason does not know.'

Thus there are indeed appropriate 'references' in common experience and scientific observation, in aesthetic appreciation and deep emotional response, which provide a grounding for religious assertions. There is also the experience of 'refreshment and companionship' to which religious people appeal and which is not to be dismissed simply on the grounds that it does not fit into some previously assumed rationalistic scheme. The result is a combination of conviction and openness. There is a tentative quality which is not the contradiction of the certitude that experience and observation provide, but rather is associated with a faith for living. We cannot make a pretentious claim to give an account of everything under and above the sun. For some of us, this more tentative approach appears more consistent with the truth stated by St Paul, that 'we walk by faith'. At the same time, there is no suggestion that such light as we do possess is to be extinguished just because we do not have complete mathematical or logical certainty.

If the model for deity is cosmic Love in action, this is exactly what one would expect to be the case. Nobody can *prove* the reality of love, not even of human love. It belongs to the dimension of lived experience and it is proved, if that is the proper word, only by living it out. We can know it to be true only by living in terms of it. It is a matter of trusting in Love and in love's working. This emphasis on love I believe to be essential. Whitehead rightly remarked years ago, 'If the modern world is to find God it must find him through love and not through fear' (*Religion in the Making*, p. 73). With such philosophical and other support as is available and possible, talk about God remains none the less exactly what the Englishman John Wesley once said about all genuine religious faith: it is 'experimental and practical'.